The Demagogue's Disease

Edward A. Morris

World Wide Products
San Francisco

Library of Congress Cataloging in Publication Data

Morris, Edward A   1925–
   The demagogue's disease.

   Includes index.
   1. Power (Social sciences) 2. Politicians.
I. Title.
JC330.M68   301.15'5   79–64157
ISBN 0–934062–00–5
ISBN 0–934062–01–3 pbk.

World Wide Products
Publications Division
740 Pine Street
San Francisco
California, 94108

To my wife Betty,
who for thirty-two years has
inspired and encouraged me.

And to all the people who have
dreamed of a better world, and
died in the struggle to achieve it.

Barbara Walters: So what do you guys do?

Senator James Abourezk (Dem., South Dakota): Well, . . . primarily we're here to run for reelection.

—ABC-TV Evening News
(October 24, 1978)

Contents

Acknowledgments

I am grateful to many for the completion of this book:

- To the former U.S. Chief of Naval Operations, Admiral Elmo R. Zumwalt, whose experiences in dealing with Congress confirmed my belief that many of its members place greater emphasis on reelection than they do on the broader national interest.
- To the former President of the Republic of the Philippines, Diosdado Macapagal, for describing his experiences with numerous heads of state.
- To Philip E. Lilienthal for pointing me in the right direction.
- To Paul Weisser for his editorial counsel and assistance.
- To Gene Ulansky for his guidance and constructive support.
- To Nat Andriani of United Press International for his help and advice in selecting photographs.
- To Dodge Crockett for his candid and critical suggestions.
- To my family for their constant assurance, particularly Marshall for his encouragement and inspiration while himself overcoming unbelievable handicaps.
- And to all those in many countries who, after confiding in me how they or relatives or friends were tortured by tyrants, asked me to help.

The Demagogue's Disease

Introduction

Most of the political turmoil in the world today can be traced back to a single source: career politicians pursuing the power and the glory associated with high political office. Though the symptoms may be mild at first, that pursuit contains within it the germs of a highly contagious and dangerous social disease. I call it the demagogue's disease.

I have been studying this disease for a number of years now, but I found very early that by observing how it operates in other cultures I could better comprehend how it drains the humanity from all of us. Thus, although this book is about political leaders, not about poverty, I think the reader will better understand my thrust if I describe a couple of personal encounters that helped me to clarify my ideas.

Knowledge from the East

I had been walking for some time along a dirt road in a country in Southeast Asia. When the road ended, I saw a small village of hovels on the other side of a creek that was spanned by a fallen tree. I carefully balanced myself on the tree and crossed over to the village. On the opposite bank, a frail little girl, clothed in rags and probably not more than five years old, came up to me. She would have been pretty had it not been for an open sore on each of her cheeks. With one hand she brushed away the gnats and flies hovering over the sores; with the other she reached out toward me in a begging gesture. I couldn't help staring at those sores. They obviously needed stitches, and I kept wondering why no one had done anything for her. Since I had no money on me, I gave her what sympathy I could and then walked further into the village.

A teenage boy who spoke some English soon undertook to guide me around. Some time later, squatting on a mat in his father's hut, we were sipping tea and talking. When the subject of medical care came up, I asked: "That little girl I saw at the bridge—how will she get her sores taken care of?"

The boy pointed to a shack off to the side of the village. It was about four feet high, perhaps six feet wide, and resembled an old packing box. "Father is dead," he said. "She lives with mother." Then he explained that her mother was very sick and had no means of support.

Seeing that I didn't grasp what the death of the girl's father had to do with her sores, he said: "Mother loves her very much. She doesn't want daughter to die. To make her beg good so she can buy rice, each night mother open sores with stick."

As I nodded that I understood, I thought of my own young daughters and uttered a silent vow to try to do something for the world's helpless children.

Throughout the next day, I was the guest of several high-ranking military officials. In the morning, the wife of one of them took me on a tour of the city in her chauffeur-driven, air-conditioned Mercedes. When we pulled into a gas station, several beggars hobbled toward the car and extended their hands. My hostess wrinkled her nose in their direction and said: "Often those beggars deform one another so they'll look pathetic. I wouldn't give them a thing; it will just encourage them."

She was right about beggars being deformed to look pathetic; I had learned that just the day before. Yet this practice didn't seem to bother her, nor did she seem upset by the fact that the beggars dotted the city like flies. But despite her unruffled pose, I suspected that deep down, like many of the wealthy in the world, she wished to improve the lot of the poor but honestly didn't know where to begin. Where *does* one begin?

At the end of the day, I was chauffeured to the home of an important official to meet his family and enjoy his hospitality. His property was surrounded by a high stone wall with broken glass embedded on top of it. His neighbor's home had a high brick wall around it with coils of barbed wire on top. I learned that most wealthy families in the neighborhood maintained armed guards around the clock. Some of them were armed with submachine guns to protect the property from the poor who lived a mile away.

The next day I visited the president's sprawling palace. Its inner courtyard contained tanks and half-tracks. These expensive weapons made me think of the little beggar girl and her mother, hovering on the edge of starvation.

I began to see that the sour note in this system—indeed, in any political system—was not a question of rich versus poor, but of leadership. From examples like this, I began to conclude that a political leader, even if he* is initially concerned with the plight of the poor, will soon begin to neglect them. For, after all, the poor are easy to neglect. They are unorganized; they live at the end of a dirt road; and armed guards keep them at a safe distance.

Knowledge from the West

When I recently visited Haiti, I saw that such conditions are not limited to Southeast Asia. Let me describe what I witnessed there.

From the window of the airport taxi driving me to Port-au-

---

*I must ask the reader to forgive my occasional use of masculine pronouns to refer to politicians. My reason for this is not that most politicians are male (a situation that I hope the proposals in this book will help to correct), but I simply wish to avoid the awkward necessity of having to constantly refer to *him or her, he or she,* etc. Where possible, I have used plural forms *(they, their, them)* to bypass the problem entirely.

Prince, I saw a huge metal sign spanning the capital's main street. It read:

LONG LIVE THE PRESIDENT FOR LIFE—DUVALIER!

I had come to Haiti to see for myself how people were treated under a president-for-life. This glittering sign was my first clue.

I knew that François "Papa Doc" Duvalier, a former practicing physician, had once been outraged by the corrupt government and the poverty in his country. In 1957, he entered politics vowing to change things. Once in power, however, the doctor, like Dr. Jekyll, turned into Mr. Hyde. In fact, he soon set himself up as president-for-life and became the most ruthless leader in Haitian history. When he died, his son Jean-Claude "Baby Doc" Duvalier became president-for-life.

Now, as I drove along the main street to my hotel, the city looked well cared for; there were few signs of extreme poverty. "Driver, where do the poor people live?" I asked. He glanced over his shoulder but said nothing.

The next morning, a different cab driver answered my question. Standing beside his cab, he told me that it was against the law to take tourists into the poor sections. But after looking up and down the street to see if we were being watched, he nodded to the right.

I walked in that direction and soon came upon a woodworking factory where tourist art was made. Inside the factory, I noticed a back door that led deeper into the forbidden neighborhood. I took this opportunity, and a few blocks later came to a corner.

Then, rounding the corner, I suddenly saw hundreds of people sitting and squatting in the muddy street. Most of them were doing nothing. One woman, however, was spreading a couple of gunnysacks over an old tire. On top of the sacks she placed a little mound of rice. A few moments later, a passerby accidentally bumped the tire, and the rice spilled into the mud. I watched the woman meticulously pick all the grains from the mud, wipe them off on her dirty blouse, and put them back on the gunnysacks.

Sitting nearby were three women who had hair, skin, and ragged clothing the color of the charcoal they were selling by the handful. Perhaps their customers cooked mud-caked rice with it.

Up to now, the people in the street had been eyeing me, but no one spoke to me until a boy came up and offered to show me around. Accompanied by a guide, I appeared more approachable, and soon a crowd gathered around me. We talked for a while about where I was from and what they could sell me. Then I asked the question that had been on my mind since I arrived in the capital: "What does your president do for you?"

After the crowd briefly discussed the question among themselves, a spokesman replied: "On national holidays, his police bring pictures of him to all of us. So no matter how poor you are, you will have a picture of the president."

That is what had become of Duvalier's concern for the poor.

A Simple Device

In my travels, I have witnessed variations of such deplorable conditions in many nations. The president-for-life syndrome is only the most blatant form of the world's self-seeking and incompetent leadership. I have concluded that, sooner or later, once they get into office, politicians change: they become victims of the demagogue's disease.

Why does it happen? What goes wrong? Must it always be that way?

I will attempt to answer these questions in the following chapters. Although the disease is spreading unchecked, I believe the human race can put a stop to it, and with a relatively simple device.

But how, you may ask, can a simple cure exist for a problem that has plagued mankind for centuries? You would be right to be skeptical. I have been working on this problem for more than ten years, and I have wondered at times if I was on the right track. So I am going to ask you to bear with me as I tell you what I have seen happening in the world of politics and what I think can and should be done about it. By the end of the book, I believe you will be willing to try the cure I suggest.

Let me remind you of something that happened in the late eighteenth century. Until that time, smallpox had been a crippling, disfiguring, and often fatal disease which had plagued mankind for centuries. There was no treatment or cure for it, and sometimes a third of a nation's population died from it. Then, one day, Edward Jenner suggested that a puslike serum from a sick cow be put on a needle and jabbed into the human body. He said that if everyone followed this suggestion, eventually we would rid the world of the dangerous disease.

The problem I am addressing is every bit as severe and widespread as smallpox once was, yet the cure is every bit as simple. It requires basically one little jab at career politics. But before I describe that "jab," let us first see how the demagogue's disease works and how all of us unwittingly help to spread it.

1 | Symptoms

Whenever people get into positions of prominence, they become susceptible to the demagogue's disease. This mental condition, the desire to remain in a position of power and glory, might be described as an inflammation of the ego that causes swelling without growth. It erodes wisdom. It can strike clerks in a bureaucracy as well as kings and presidents.

Now, when non-politicians contract the disease, usually few people are harmed. But when, on the other hand, the wisdom of political leaders becomes warped, entire nations may suffer.

This chapter will briefly indicate the symptoms of the various stages of the disease. As you read on, you will probably become aware of how the disease is flourishing in your own city, state, or nation. Let's start, then, with the first-stage symptoms, the initial eruptions of egotism—or as some would call it, the emergence of political pragmatism.

First-Stage Symptoms

To put it charitably, politicians tend to be immodest. Since they are continually running for office, they take to heart the advice found in Gilbert and Sullivan's musical, *Ruddigore* (1887):

> *If you wish in the world to advance*
> *Your merits you're bound to enhance.*
> *You must stir it and stump it*
> *And blow your own trumpet,*
> *Or, trust me, you haven't a chance.*

We have all noticed that when politicians speak they constantly boast of their accomplishments. Even politicians who try to appear unpretentious make sure that their unpretentiousness is well advertised. For example, when President Carter wears denims, the White House stresses that fact to prove he is just like us. California's Governor Jerry Brown even got political mileage from driving an old Plymouth and sleeping on a mattress on the floor.

There is, in fact, too much show business in politics, and an occasional politician will even admit it. In a television interview on October 24, 1978, ABC News Correspondent Barbara Walters asked Senator James Abourezk (Dem., South Dakota) about the United States Senate: "So what do you guys do?" The candid senator replied: "Well, we run for reelection and we in effect go into show business and do what we can to get press."* Being in "show business," politicians become overly concerned with keeping up their image for the folks back home. In fact, maintaining that good image soon begins to take precedence over maintaining the good of the people.

Image-conscious politicians like to dodge controversial issues by passing the buck to the courts or to future generations. But when that isn't feasible, they use other ploys. One is to spread responsibility around. Political columnist Dick Nolan, writing in the *San Francisco Examiner* (March 7, 1978), explains how this device works:

> When a politician has a tricky problem to deal with, one containing a lot of potential for disaster, the smartest thing he can do is to involve a lot of other people in it. That way, no matter what happens, he can take bows for accomplishments, or, if things turn out badly, can dilute the blame to the vanishing

---

*Copyright by the American Broadcasting Companies, Inc., 1978. Reprinted by permission.

point. The mechanism for accomplishing all these
things is the citizens committee.

"Just exactly what do you propose to do about
this, Senator?"

"Glad you asked that, son. I propose to take
steps immediately to appoint a small citizens committee. . . ."

In addition to evasive acts, most politicians quickly learn to
use evasive words. As Governor Jerry Brown once remarked about
politics: "A little vagueness goes a long way in this business."

The immodesty and the excessive concern with image, the
first-stage symptoms of the demagogue's disease, become worse the
longer a politician stays in power. When the image he has created
becomes so important to him that he neglects the problems he was
elected to deal with, stage one turns into the narcissism of stage
two.

Second-Stage Symptoms

The politician likes to see his image wherever he looks. In recent
years, the presidents of more than two dozen nations, all presumably elected for a specified term, have ordered their own faces
imprinted on the national currency or stamps. Among these countries are Taiwan, Egypt, Indonesia, the Philippines, Ghana, the
Dominican Republic, and Uganda.

Unfortunately, this symptom is not confined to stamps and
money. Even American presidents have permitted their photographs to hang in every federal office and post office in the land. In
the Dominican Republic, when an army recruit makes his bed, it
is his duty to place a photograph of the country's president on his
pillow. In an even more blatant display of narcissism, President Idi
Amin Dada of Uganda ordered 60,000 T-shirts with his likeness on
them to be distributed to his countrymen.

> *That government is the strongest of which*
> *every man feels himself a part.*
>
> —Thomas Jefferson, 1807

When a politician cannot constantly have his face before the public, he may elect to have his name do the job. Many American mayors add their names to the welcome signs at the borders of their cities, as if it weren't enough to greet the visitors with the sign simply reading, for example, "Welcome to the City of San Francisco."

Another example of this kind of narcissism is the legislators' habit of introducing useless or overlapping bills simply to keep their names before the public. Legislators who don't draft their own bills often engage in "tomb stoning," that is, having their names added to bills as if they were co-authors. Mervyn Dymally, California's former Lieutenant Governor, told me that this practice helps feed a politician's ego. It also helps make constituents believe their representatives are doing something.

The edifice complex is another narcissistic symptom. Politicians commonly name public buildings, parks, or fountains after themselves, or they may put statues of themselves in as many public places as possible. Such monuments can be highly ephemeral, however. Kwame Nkrumah of Ghana and the Shah of Iran both erected statues of themselves all over their countries, but none of them is still standing.

Third-Stage Symptoms

When the politician starts to distort reality, the symptoms have grown more severe. In Uganda, Idi Amin tried to create an illusion of prosperity by ordering stores to display empty boxes in their windows so as to make it appear that goods were plentiful. Some politicians, as George Orwell accurately forecast, even rewrite history. For example, ever since the publication of his memoirs, Soviet President Leonid Brezhnev has emerged in his country's press as one of World War II's great heroes.

When a narcissistic politician begins dallying with the trappings of royalty, it is another sure sign that he is further removing himself from the down-to-earth problems of his people. Jean Bedel Bokassa, who proclaimed himself Emperor Bokassa I of the Central African Empire, provides a recent example. Like Napoleon, Emperor Bokassa placed the crown on his own head. His coronation, in December 1977, cost his underdeveloped nation one-fourth of its annual earnings from all exports. On a somewhat smaller but still grand scale, President Mobuto of Zaire once ordered $60,000 worth of Coca-Cola flown in from the U.S. for a party.

Extravagance, of course, has long been a prerogative of absolute monarchs, and the practice continues right into the present. In 1978, for example, King Khaled of Saudi Arabia had the Netherlands build for him a 212-foot yacht costing $14 million, the most luxurious yacht ever built. In addition to its three decks, including a helicopter platform, it has an operating room with an intensive care unit, closed-circuit television, a swimming pool, a sauna, a barbershop, and a gymnasium. All the fixtures are gold-plated.

Lavishness is also no stranger to American politicians. Even former U.S. Secretary of the Treasury William E. Simon, who was regarded as the Ford administration's foremost critic of excessive government spending, wound up a victim of this syndrome. When Simon left in November 1976 for a trip to Moscow, he intended to take along only his wife and two sons. In addition to them, however, he found himself being accompanied by a government party of forty-two, which included a retinue of aides, secretaries, and other assistants, and more than a dozen Secret Service agents. Whether or not such junkets are expensive or unnecessary is not what I'm

> *While all other sciences have advanced, that of government is at a standstill—little better understood, little better practised now than three or four thousand years ago.*
>
> —John Adams, 1813

concerned about, however. I'm interested in what they do to the politician's ego.

It is amazing how often politicians feel that rules applicable to the rest of us don't apply to them. Rulers of various countries continually resort to locking up critics of their regimes as President Marcos of the Philippines and President Park of South Korea have done. In his *Memoirs*, former President Nixon stood by his claim that an illegal act becomes legal if committed by the President. Unfortunately, he has no less an authority than Plato to support his claim, for Plato wrote in *The Republic* that "if anyone at all is to have the privilege of lying, the rulers of the state should be such persons."

This concept that leaders make the rules but don't necessarily have to follow them was dramatized by Shakespeare. In *Henry V*, when Kate refuses the king a kiss on the lips, she explains that it is not the fashion for maids in France to kiss before they are married. The king replies: "Oh, Kate, nice customs curtsy to great Kings. Dear Kate, you and I cannot be confined within the weak list of a country's fashion; we are the makers of manners, Kate."

But even more repugnant than a leader's regal conduct are his identifications with divinity—or what we might call the demigod's disease. For centuries the world has lived with the notion that its leaders have been touched by divinity. In the United States, of course, this notion is seldom expressed other than in biblical rhetoric. For example, President Woodrow Wilson implied that he, like

Jesus, would drive the moneylenders from the temple. In less open societies, even stronger assertions can be made. Two recent examples spring to mind. One came from President Idi Amin, who claimed that the death in a car crash of the Anglican archbishop of Uganda was a "punishment of God" because the archbishop had dared to speak out against Amin. The other example came from former Prime Minister Eric Gairy of Grenada, who claimed that God chose him to raise his tiny island nation to greatness. A fortune-teller once told him that "a little man shall come from the East." The 5 foot 7 inch tall Gairy, who was born on the eastern side of the island, said: "I am that man. It was all arranged long before I was born. . . ."

Fourth-Stage Symptoms

Most politicians find the combination of power and glory so addicting that they never wish to give it up. Look at the ages of some recent world leaders. Were there so few young political leaders in Taiwan that Chiang Kai-shek had to be "reelected" at the age of 86? Was Ireland so devoid of younger political leaders that the nation had to choose between a 68-year-old contender and a 91-year-old president (de Valera) running for yet another six-year term? Did Spain have no one more qualified to settle its unrest than 81-year-old Generalissimo Franco? When politicians get power, they contend that they are the only ones who can solve society's problems. Few of them groom successors, because they don't want to let challengers rise to the surface.

In fact, politicians will go to almost any lengths to remain in office. Where constitutional limits about succession cannot be changed, politicians have dredged up ingenious schemes to ouflank the law. For example, when he became ineligible for reelection because of his state's constitution, Alabama's Governor George Wallace had his wife Lurleen run for governor. A variation of this

> *No man is good enough to govern another*
> *man without that other's consent.*
>
> —Abraham Lincoln, 1854

is the phenomenon of the leader arranging for some member of his family to inherit his "elective" position. In Argentina, when Juan Peron died, his wife Isabel, a former dancer, became president. Similarly, Mrs. Imelda Marcos, a former beauty queen and now the governor of metropolitan Manila, is first in line to succeed her husband as president of the Philippines.

It is no wonder that there is so much loss of faith in politicians and political institutions in almost every country of the world. Even in the United States, the Proposition 13 tax revolt that began in California in 1978 and quickly swept across the country was in part a response to the incompetence of career politicians. These are the very people who are so quick to contend that only they, with their long political experience, can make the system work. In fact, they are the very reason it doesn't work.

In the following chapter, we will see how the disease that affects career politicians undermines their ability to make *any* system work.

"Let's see, it should sound hopeful, responsible, gubernatorial and more than a little presidential."

2 | Course of the Disease

Imagine that you are an entertainer with your name constantly in lights. Imagine also that millions idolize you. After performing before heads of state and dining with royalty, you are bound to feel a cut above less celebrated mortals. No doubt, you would feel very reluctant to give it all up and go back home.

Something similar happens to politicians. They, too, are human. I'm not suggesting that they all become corrupt or evil. Some work selflessly for their people. Unfortunately, most of them believe that by virtue of their selflessness they should stay in office indefinitely. There are endless examples of excellent human beings —intelligent and benevolent—who come to power eager to do what is best for their people. But they rarely succeed—at least, not for long. The high rate of failure is proportionate to the length of time they remain in office. The more time that passes, the more they are shaped by the ego massage which is part of the glory of office.

How It Begins

Consider what a typical political leader must experience within. It doesn't make any difference what country he is in or what political system he is a part of. From the moment he is given his new title —Prime Minister, Commissar, or President—he starts to change. He can't help it.

In the case of lesser officials, it happens this way. First of all, the politician's position often includes a number of fringe benefits.

18

Individually they are insignificant, but they become a pattern of life. For example, he receives free medical and dental care, free mailing privileges, free parking, free passes to sporting events, and meals in fashionable restaurants where he is never permitted to pick up a check. He also is given honorariums for speeches and receives gifts from new friends—from cases of champagne to jewelry and works of art. New friends may also help him to buy stock at the right time or to purchase land at a fraction of its true value.

Gradually, psychological changes in the politician begin to mirror the material ones. As a senator or congressman, he is constantly in demand and feels it. Famous or important persons seek his advice or help, and his supporters hang on his every word and encourage him to hold forth. Soon he becomes the victim of such attention and finds it very easy to believe that his words *are* important.

When protocol dictates that a leader ride at the head of every parade and sit in a seat of honor at banquets, there is a tremendous tendency for him to believe that such honors are his due. It is very difficult for him to keep his feet on the ground when he is the center of attraction at military parades, when Secret Service men rush to open doors for him, and when he is on a first-name basis with the superstars of national and international politics.

The Role of the Media

From the very beginning, the media also feed the leader's ego. His smiles, gestures, and mannerisms become media events, since television viewers and newspaper readers generally prefer personalities to issues. As the leader grows accustomed to the click of cameras and the pop of flashbulbs, he eventually learns to manipulate the media. During a campaign, for example, he may stage a rally in an auditorium deliberately chosen because it is too small; that way it will appear on TV as if it were bursting with his supporters.

In Canada, since the House of Commons began to televise
its hearings in 1976, there has developed what is known as the
"Commons Shuffle." When one member rises to speak, the other
members move in to fill the empty seats around him in order to get
their own faces on television.

The problem is that we choose our leaders to think about our
interests, but then we make those leaders into performers who
think instead about makeup and image. While it may be true that
applause and cheers can make an actor more dramatic, a gymnast
more agile, or a boxer more powerful, they do not make a politician
more wise.

Inner Circling

As we make more demands on politicians, they must justifiably
increase their staffs.* But as their staffs increase in size, the politicians can't help magnifying their feelings of self-importance. President Carter has a staff of 351. Mrs. Carter has a staff of 17, who plan
engagements, answer requests, and keep her briefed. During his
second term (1936–1940), President Franklin Roosevelt had a staff
of 55; his wife Eleanor, one of the most active presidential wives in
history, got by with only three aides. What is really remarkable is
that during FDR's first presidential campaign he criticized President Hoover's "excessively large staff" of four aides!

Extensive staffs and a theatrical orientation tend to hinder
the politician's dialogue with the public. So do the effects of highly
orchestrated campaign trips designed to avoid hecklers using clev-
erly worded questions which could tarnish the leader's image. So

---

*In 1949 each congressman had three staff members, but by 1979 each had a staff of eighteen.
According to Carter Manasco, a 77-year-old former congressman from Alabama: "In 1948
the House Appropriations Committee had the largest staff on the Hill—four. Now, hell, the
District of Columbia Committee, which didn't report a major bill in the last Congress, has
43 staffers and some are paid as much as $50,000 a year." (See Paul Houston and John H.
Averill, "The Ever-Expanding Staff for Congress," *Los Angeles Times*, April 6, 1979. Copyright © 1979 by the Los Angeles Times. Reprinted by permission.)

> *The less government we have the better.*
>
> —Ralph Waldo Emerson, 1841

he gradually becomes less open and accessible. He may avoid prob-
ing reporters and fiery leaders of equal rank. His news conferences
may become increasingly structured, and his conversations with
the public increasingly one-sided. As he ages, he may isolate himself
from the confusion and threat of crowds, withdrawing more and
more within the small circle of aides and close supporters.

Insecure leaders stage appearances at out-of-the-way military bases, for the audiences of military personnel and their families
would never think of publicly expressing dissatisfaction. Unfortunately, by protecting his image, a politician can lose touch with his
own people. Unwittingly he may create effective filters between
himself and the rest of us. In *The Life and Times of W. H. Taft*
(Hamden, Conn.: Archon Books, 1964, p. 558), Henry Pringle de-
scribes how easily a leader may end up hearing only good news:

> The acoustics of a special train bearing the President
> of the United States are notoriously bad. The Presi-
> dent is told only good news by the politicians, yearn-
> ing for favors, who crowd aboard. The voices of
> protest are drowned in the applause of those who
> swarm to see the circus.

Speaking of trains, I am reminded of a story about Mahatma
Gandhi which illustrates how a leader's supporters can isolate him
from the public even at those moments when he thinks he has come
closest to the people. It seems that when Gandhi traveled around
India by train, he always insisted upon riding in the section with the
poorest peasants and beggars. Now, you might think that was a

highly admirable idea and one auguring well for India's democratic future. But what actually happened? According to one account (Larry Collins and Dominique Lapierre, *Freedom at
Midnight* [New York: Simon & Schuster, 1975], p. 103), "Lord
Mountbatten asked one of Gandhi's closest associates, the poetess
Sarojini Naidu, whether, in view of the determined poverty in
which Gandhi chose to live, the Congress Party could really protect
him. 'Ah,' she said, laughing, 'you and Gandhi may imagine that
when he walks down that Calcutta station platform looking for a
suitably crowded third-class car that he's alone. . . . What he doesn't
know is that there are a dozen of our people dressed as Untoucha-
bles walking behind him, crowding into that car. . . . My dear Lord
Louis, . . . you will never know how much it has cost the Congress
Party to keep that old man in poverty.' "

    Admittedly, this kind of detachment from reality on the
leader's part was relatively harmless, both for Gandhi and the Indian people. Much more serious was the way the later Gandhi,
Prime Minister Indira Gandhi, was cut off from the feelings of the
Indian people. You may recall Mrs. Gandhi's shock when the Indian
electorate voted her out of office in 1977. Her advisers, it was later
discovered, were reluctant to warn her how unpopular she was
becoming. The same thing apparently happened to the Shah of
Iran, who, after his ouster, told President Sadat of Egypt: "My
advisers built a wall between myself and my people. I didn't realize
what was happening. When I woke up, I had lost my people" (*Time*,
February 5, 1979, p. 110).

    Why does a staff filter the news to the leader? Often mem-
bers of the staff and others close to the seat of power tend to do this
because they desire to keep their jobs. They often overlook graft
and refrain from "blowing the whistle," since that, too, would jeop-
ardize their positions. Furthermore, they may also work to suppress
open dissent. If dissent were allowed to reach the boiling point,
then a leader might demand the resignation of one of his aides to
quiet the protests.

> *We do not elect our wisest and best men to represent us in the Senate and the Congress. In general, we elect men of the type that subscribes to only one principle—to get reelected.*
>
> —Terry M. Townsend, 1940

Tyrants frequently keep their staff members fighting among themselves so none become too strong or build up a following. While this practice may keep staff members from joining together to stage a coup, it also keeps them from addressing the problems under their jurisdiction, and the results can be disastrous for the country.

Addiction

The effects of these conditions create a different man from the one who first came to power, though the veneer may be the same. He begins to show more zest for bronzing his footprints in the dust behind him than for tackling the problems he originally seemed so concerned about. By this point, politics has become the only career he can conceive of. Loss of power means forfeiting the excitement or the livelihood he has become accustomed to and so greatly enjoys. So he campaigns incessantly. The late Congressman Leo Ryan of California candidly admitted that those in Congress normally spend about ten months of every two-year term doing nothing but campaigning.

An ongoing campaign needs a constant flow of funds, so the leader gives a ready ear to the requests of his principal financial backers. Compromise becomes easier. Though he may never cross the invisible line into outright dishonesty, he will find it increas-

ingly more difficult to take an unpopular stand. A strong position
may alienate blocs of voters. So he finds it easier to sidestep the real
problems of mankind such as crime, pollution, inflation, overpopulation, political terrorism, a balanced budget, the arms race, and the
energy crisis.

In the United States, as I've indicated earlier, the leader
might try to avoid an explosive issue by maneuvering it into the
courts or by trying to pass it on to future generations. The crisis in
America's Social Security system, which had to be bailed out
through large increases in payroll taxes, is an example of the
present paying the price for past political sidestepping.

The Erosion of Wisdom

Wisdom alone does not immunize one against the demagogue's
disease. It is my contention that long careers of power and glory will
sap the wisdom from even the greatest minds. Once the leader's
wisdom has eroded, his thinking takes some strange turns. To re-
concile his new image with our expectations of him, he may
become less than candid. He may rationalize the deception, argu-
ing that his true opinion would make him less effective in bringing
about positive changes. This posture makes it easier for him to be
less truthful in the future. President Gerald Ford called this approach "political license."

A leader may begin to claim credit for any improvement
that has occurred during his tenure of office. For example, if an
unusually mild weather cycle has led to bumper crops, he will take
credit for the prosperity. He might make the equally fallacious
argument that he ought to be reelected because of his years of
experience in politics. Much of his so-called experience, however,
consists of self-aggrandizement and political bargaining for favor
and position.

Underlying his faulty logic is the fear of having to seek another job. A Washington, D.C., executive recruiting firm reports that corporate personnel officers are not very interested in hiring former top government officials. The reasons given are that "government service is an unreal world," and such tenure in Washington "is of little use in the business world." Those in government, say the personnel officers, "fail to show sufficient concern about costs and are spoiled by the perquisites of power: from limos to swimming pools to junkets around the world."*

Such spoiled politicians, furthermore, gradually develop contempt for their original constituencies as they concern themselves first and foremost with rising from office to office. In 1976, Congressman John R. Rhodes (Rep., Arizona) said: "A large number of congressmen are cynical, abrasive, frequently uncommunicative, and ambitious to an inordinate degree. In their eagerness to draw attention to themselves—and advance politically—they frustrate the legislative process." The congressman's description of his colleagues adds up to a pretty fair diagnosis of what happens to just about anyone after a prolonged exposure to the demagogue's disease.

Quoted from the *San Francisco Examiner,* December 21, 1977. Reprinted by permission of The Chicago Daily News and Field Enterprises, Inc.

3 | Chronic Illness

Given the fearful fate of numerous leaders of the world—assassination, the firing squad, the gallows, prison—it is understandable why so many of them will go to any lengths to stay in power. By so doing they set in motion a vicious circle which all of their people get caught up in. This chapter will explore that chronic condition which exists at this very moment in nearly one hundred member countries of the United Nations.

A Vicious Circle

A typical circle might begin with a leader restoring "law and order" by declaring martial law—which means that he suppresses dissent. It now becomes a crime to challenge his authority. Those who do —students, writers, clergy, and even potential rivals—are jailed indefinitely. Friends and relatives who protest the jailings are themselves imprisoned. Then, in desperation, someone resorts to violence to strike back at the oppressive regime. Attempts are made on the lives of the oppressors; whether successful or not, the government responds with counter-terrorism, including torture. This in turn incites even greater dissent, including aid by exiles to any underground movement pledged to overthrow the tyrant.

As large segments of the people become the enemy of the government, business confusion develops and eventually economic chaos ensues. Then, as the nation's problems get out of hand, the military—and this is a worldwide pattern—become disgusted with the leader's mismanagement. Eventually, they oust the incompetent leader, explaining that they had to clean up the mess created by the politicians.

Because the deposed tyrant had eliminated potential rivals and driven many of the skilled and professional citizens into exile, there is a dearth of leadership. The leader of the coup, probably a colonel or general, soon decides that he is the best one suited to run the government. Because of his military training, however, he is usually even less tolerant than his predecessor. Furthermore, owing to the economic upheaval that preceded the coup, the new leader faces an even more difficult economic situation than existed before his takeover; for as the coup began to appear likely, many of the wealthy citizens started sending their capital out of the country. This, in turn, rapidly weakened the economy and helped precipitate the coup.

Before long, the new leader, no more able to solve the problems of his country than was his predecessor, finds that he, too, must resort to martial law and suppress dissent in order to stay in power. So the citizens' younger brothers and sisters end up fighting and dying to remove the very tyrant whom their older brothers and sisters had once hailed as a liberator and fought and died for. It's just a vicious circle.

Further Complications

One further complication is the military belief that the best interests of the nation are served by a strong armed forces. Therefore, when the military leaders are in complete control, it is only natural that they will divert a great part of the nation's budget to military expenditures. So in the vicious circle we're referring to, we find that the military, which may have taken power to alleviate economic chaos, have by their military appropriations further aggravated a faltering economy.

Take the case of Peru. During 1978, the prices of gasoline, bread, milk, and flour jumped more than 50 percent. President

Francisco Morales Bermudez, a retired general, proposed austerity measures. However, the military leaders opposed having their budget cut. They also opposed Morales' liberal policies: strengthening civil and human rights, permitting political broadcasts, and allowing a relatively uncensored press. Morales failed to persuade his former military colleagues to accept austerity; so, in order to stay in office, he yielded to their wishes. With a greater military budget, inflation increased, the masses suffered more, and Morales started to lose civilian support. The people were soon agreeing with the agitators opposed to the regime. But instead of attacking inflation and thereby angering the military, Morales charged that Peru faced "an organized subversive movement." Then he declared a state of emergency and suspended constitutional guarantees of assembly and free speech. Newspapers were ordered closed, political broadcasts were banned, and elections were postponed.

Morales' declaration had become a self-fulfilling prophecy: by May 1978, police in Lima were firing on rock-throwing rioters, and bodies started to fall on all sides.

Under martial law, without normal checks on his power, a leader becomes more susceptible than ever to the ruthlessness of the demagogue's disease. In South Korea, for example, President Park Chung Hee condemned a poet to death who had criticized him in a poem. In Ethiopia, the military council which overthrew Emperor Haile Selassie promised "a democratic form of government." However, three months after the coup, the council executed its chairman, Lieutenant General Aman Michael Andom, for acting as tyranically as the deposed emperor.

Once in power, leaders use various ruses to legitimize martial law. The most common is the referendum, which incidentally is an excellent device for quieting complaints from the U.S. State Department. No matter what the referendum's outcome, the leader always remains in power. Even if a fairly worded referendum goes against him, he can proudly point to his regime's free elections. Then he'll announce that he has learned how strongly his

> *I think we have more machinery of government than is necessary, too many parasites living on the labor of the industrious.*
>
> —Thomas Jefferson, 1824

people feel about a certain problem which he says he will correct within the next few years.

In some so-called elections, the leader's name is the only one on the ballot. Since most voters prefer the devil they know to some unknown devil, they usually vote "yes." For example, Ferdinand Marcos has held five referendums since he imposed martial law on the Philippines in 1972. With no opposition candidates allowed on the ballot, with non-voting made a crime, and with any village casting a large "no" vote soon finding that its government-sponsored projects are transferred to villages that cast large "yes" votes, Marcos has won almost 90 percent of the vote each time.

After the United States condemned Chile for violating human rights, the South American country's ruling junta branded the condemnation an act of "international aggression" and set up a referendum asking the electorate to affirm them in such loaded language that a negative vote would have been virtually unpatriotic. After receiving 75 percent of the vote, President Pinochet said that Chile needed "no more elections or votings or consultations for ten more years."

Terror and Counter-Terror

Under martial law, with no chance of fairly challenging the leaders, the oppressed often resort to terror. I have talked with people imprisoned and tortured by dictators, and I can understand their common desire to strike back and destroy the tyrant.

I think we Americans would react the same way, and I so testified in Washington before the Congressional Subcommittee on International Organizations, in June 1975. Think about this for a moment: Suppose that at a time of great discontent in our nation, our President declares martial law to restore "law and order." Assume further that some congressmen protest the imposition of martial law and the suspension of our Constitution, and so the President jails them.

It is reasonable to assume that still more members of Congress, who have previously been silent, might object to the jailing of their colleagues. At that point, the President orders Congress closed. Henceforth, he will attend to the legislative as well as the executive decisions of our country.

Now, some of the students who were incarcerated for opposing martial law are tortured and die in jail. Many of our religious leaders begin to speak out against abuses of human rights, and they, too, are jailed.

As the months of martial law in our country roll into years, and as the President continues to give excuses for the suspension of the Constitution and even starts talking about having his wife take over when he dies, would you not expect more Americans to join with others in working for the eventual overthrow of such a demagogue?

How long would you expect Americans to tolerate the closing of Congress and the suspension of our Constitution before they started forming coalitions to restore our freedoms? One would expect that many of our military would be loyal enough to the concept of American freedom that they, too, would join in opposition to the tyrannical President.

Now add one other element. Suppose that another nation gives tremendous military and economic support to the very demagogue you are trying to unseat. Wouldn't you expect that Americans would develop a hatred for that foreign power which

> *The greatest baseness of man is his seeking for glory.*
>
> —Blaise Pascal, 1670

interferes with the political processes of the United States? Wouldn't you expect some of us to become frustrated in our attempts to unseat the tyrant? Resort to violence would be inevitable.

Of course, this is a hypothetical case for America; but it depicts the reality of the Philippines.

It is difficult for us in America to understand the desperation of people who have been tortured or whose friends or relatives have been tortured or killed at the hands of a despotic government. If these victims cannot attack the man responsible for their pain and humiliation, they often attack symbols of his authority—public buildings, statues, palaces, electrical power plants, etc. These attacks on symbols of authority elicit paranoid fears in all heads of state. All world leaders, and particularly those outside the democracies, know that other rulers have been jailed, executed, exiled, or disgraced.

We often forget that scores of countries have imprisoned their former heads of state. Many of us, for example, have forgotten that the former president of Greece, George Popodopoulos, is serving a life sentence for abuse of power. Similar or worse fates have been handed out to such notables as Ethiopia's Emperor Haile Selassie, Argentina's President Isabel Peron, Pakistan's Prime Minister Zulfikar Ali Bhutto, and many others. In fact, one nation, Benin, has *three* of its former presidents in prison.

The leader knows that the source of his downfall may come from within his own government (as was the case with President Nkrumah of Ghana) or from a mass uprising (as was the case with the Shah of Iran). In either case, because of the fear and anxiety in

most leaders, they are unable to adequately devote their full attention to the problems of their people. Instead, their usual knee-jerk
response is to resort to violence themselves. They may train additional police, impose a more restrictive curfew, and even further
curtail criticism of the government. Moreover, the authorities contend that the dissidents' violence shows the need for continuing
martial law—and counter-terror.

Some governments even use terror on nationals living
beyond their borders. Chile's secret police have killed political ref-
ugees throughout the world, including right in the center of Washington, D.C. In Los Angeles's Korean community, systematic
intimidation by the KCIA (Korean Central Intelligence Agency) is
the rule. And dissident exiles from Communist nations have been
the recent targets of poison-tipped umbrellas on the streets of London.

These days counter-terrorism is big business. One London
firm sells training courses in counter-terror. Its clients include
Cuba, the Soviet Union, Kuwait, Kenya, Nigeria, and India, who
buy courses in silent killing, basic and advanced sabotage, eaves-
dropping, and interrogation.

"Interrogation" is today's euphemism for torture. We've all
heard about Hitler's concentration camps and Stalin's Gulag Ar-
chipelago, but torture is by no means a German or Russian monopoly. France systematically used torture during its futile war in
Algeria; and in Vietnam the Saigon regime tortured suspected
Communists on a routine basis, often by placing them in inhuman
"tiger cages" with bars on all *six* sides. Investigators from Amnesty
International, the Nobel-prize-winning human rights organization,
have found that between 1966 and 1976 torture was practiced
semiofficially in sixty countries. (Individual country reports are
available from Amnesty International, 304 West 58th Street, New
York, NY 10019.) Today, experts in torture exchange their knowledge, and the latest improvements in torture technology are exported.

> *When glory comes, loss of memory follows.*
>
> —French proverb

Two of the regimes most notorious for their use of torture have been Chile under Pinochet and Iran under the Shah. In Chile, according to *Time* magazine (August 16, 1976, p. 32), the secret police are "fairly ecumenical in finding victims; former parliamentarians and army officers have been tortured, as well as suspect leftist terrorists." One such victim, a former lieutenant in the Chilean army, who was arrested by the junta after he tried to resign his commission, was quoted by *Time* as follows:

> I was tortured with electric shock, forced to live in underground dungeons so small that in one I could only stand up and in the other only lie down. I was beaten incessantly, dragged before a mock firing squad, and regularly told that my wife and child and relatives were suffering the same fate.

The intensity of the reaction against the Shah of Iran may be explained in part by the deeds of SAVAK, the former Iranian secret police, which unfortunately received much of its training from the American CIA. "The country's repertory of tortures," wrote *Time* (August 16, 1976), "includes not only electric shock and beatings but also the insertion of bottles in the rectum, hanging weights from testicles, rape, and such apparatus as a helmet that, worn over the head of the victim, magnifies his own screams."

In Equatorial Guinea, political prisoners have had eyes gouged out. Others have been forced to stand for days in a pit, up to their necks in mud and water. In Uganda, prisoners have been made to smash the heads of fellow prisoners with sledgehammers, then lie in the human debris and await their turn to have their own heads smashed in.

Aside from its atrocious inhumanity, such violence should be objectionable to its practitioners because it fails to achieve its aims. As Martin Luther King pointed out, the ultimate weakness of violence is that it begets the very thing it seeks to destroy. Thus, instead of wiping out opposition, counter-terrorism only keeps the vicious circle going round and round.

"Did You Say The Magic Words, 'Law And Order'?"

—from *Herblock's State of the Union* (Simon & Schuster, 1972)

4 | Complications

Our century has witnessed a knowledge explosion. The technological changes resulting from it have produced problems which our forefathers never dreamed of. But these technological changes have not just caused technical problems for our leaders: as I shall demonstrate, technology actually dictates the type of leaders that are chosen, and it plays a significant role in determining how long they remain in power.

The problems cry out for the wisdom of Solomon, a quality noticeably lacking in most world leaders. In fact, because of the types of leaders that are produced, the problems are aggravated. There are times when I would agree with Aldous Huxley's observation that "technological progress has merely provided us with more efficient means for going backwards."

Bureaucratic Complications

In the last fifty years, the money available for governments to spend has aggravated an undesirable quality in our leaders. They now think they are more important than they really are. But wait! They *are* more important than leaders were fifty years ago. The establishment of the income tax explains why politicians play a greater role in more of society's activities than ever before. As its coffers fill, government expands by creating new and larger bureaucracies, which tend to further overregulate us. At the present time, total spending at all government levels in the United States amounts to 40 percent of the national income.

Bureaucracies overregulate because politicians, eager to woo certain segments of the electorate, pass "enabling legislation," which merely sets up a regulatory authority. From this point on, because politicians are involved with innumerable activities, they lack the time to oversee the newly created agencies. Accordingly, many agencies are free to design and enforce their own regulations, or to show favoritism, and the whole policing apparatus becomes worse than what it was designed to correct.

Politicians find bureaucracies useful for avoiding issues and creating patronage. For the rest of us, the results are unnecessary frustration and economic stagnation. Today, American business constantly digs itself out from under an avalanche of red tape, nuisance taxes, and bureaucratically generated forms and paperwork which few bureaucrats ever read.

In 1977, Americans paid over $100 billion in order to comply with or escape from government regulations; the steel industry, for instance, had to comply with 5,600 regulations administered by hundreds of paper shufflers from twenty-six different agencies.

"Before I became President," Jimmy Carter said in April 1978, "I realized and was warned that dealing with the federal bureaucracy would be one of the worst problems I would have to face. It's been even worse than I anticipated."

Because bureaucrats are notoriously inflexible, we often see absurd applications of rules. You all know of such examples. My favorite is the agency which fined a contractor for refusing to make his construction workers wear bulky life jackets while working on a bridge over a channel. The agency refused to take into consideration that all the water had been diverted away from the bridge during the entire construction period.

The only ones who really profit from this trend toward overregulation are the lawyers. In fact, in the United States the legal profession has recently been growing at an astonishing rate. Today, there are half a million lawyers in this country—nearly three times as many as there were thirty years ago, even though the overall population has less than doubled in that time.

What these figures mean, according to *San Francisco Chronicle* columnist Charles McCabe (October 31, 1978), is that the United States has four times as many lawyers as Great Britain, five times as many as West Germany, ten times as many as France, and twenty times as many as Japan. In fact, this country has two-thirds of all the lawyers on Earth, and thousands upon thousands of potential lawyers are clamoring to get into law schools. In the words of Chief Justice Warren Burger, "We may be on our way to a society overrun by hordes of lawyers hungry as locusts."

This profusion of lawyers might be an acceptable price for society to pay if it really helped to make our lives simpler and more problem-free. Unfortunately, that's not the case. As the old story goes, there was once a small town that had only one lawyer, and he had so little work that he was almost starving. Then one day another lawyer moved into town—and before long, *both* of them were rich!

As Will Rogers once noted, "The minute you read something you can't understand, you can almost be sure it was drawn up by a lawyer." Their talent for obfuscation comes in handy when lawyers administer bureaucracies or when they go into politics— and let us not forget that most politicians come from the ranks of the lawyers.

In any case, lawyers *in* politics promote, and lawyers *out of* politics benefit from, these unfeeling and unproductive bureaucracies that quietly stifle our economy. But something just as bad, if not quite so obvious, occurs because of scientific and technological advances.

Scientific and Technological Complications

Through science and technology—that is, through better sanitation and improved medical techniques—fewer infants die at birth today than was once the case, and people in general are living longer.

> *Politics is too serious a matter to be left to the politicians.*
>
> —Charles de Gaulle, 1962

Consequently, the world's population is now increasing at the rate of 250,000 per day, 7.7 million per month, or 90 million per year.

All of the additional infants must have adequate nutrition to develop into normal human beings. Unfortunately, the misdirected priorities of most political leaders worsen the lot of their citizens. Where a daily vitamin A capsule could wipe out nutritionally caused blindness among infants, leaders instead spend untold millions on military equipment. On the other hand, as far as their own medical care is concerned, world leaders demand and receive the finest. They can therefore remain in office—alive, if not always alert—into their seventies and eighties.

I recently asked Prime Minister Morarji Desai of India, who was 83 at the time, why so many nations have leaders in their seventies and eighties. It was a good sign, he told me, explaining that since older people have more wisdom than younger ones, it showed that society was seeking wisdom. Then he paused and smiled: "But one must watch for the possibility that an older leader may become dotty."

With all respect for Desai, I must point out that leaders in their seventies and eighties are *not* in office because the public seeks out their wisdom. In most cases, society chose them when they were young, and those young leaders successfully schemed to keep themselves in office even after they became old. That's where medical science is again responsible, because more politicians are able to live longer than they would have a hundred years ago. Thus, while older politicians may think of themselves as vintage wine, most have turned to vinegar, and that's why the world is becoming so embittered.

Another technological advance with political ramifications is improved electronic communications. Even in the remotest villages in the world, the ineptness of world leadership is made known by inexpensive battery-operated transistor radios. Persons in such villages learn almost weekly that, in one country or another, peasants, workers, students, and military leaders, by their protests and riots, occasionally overthrow a government. The villagers also discover how wretched their own existence is in comparison with the rest of the world. So when their own leader's mismanagement becomes evident, even traditionally submissive peasants are now moved to protest. This means that the political leaders must divert more and more of their country's wealth to internal military and police forces.

At the same time, via daily radio news reports, desperate villagers learn about violent techniques that have overthrown a leader on the other side of the world. Often they apply those techniques at home in the belief that anything which replaces the incompetent or oppressive government they now live under would be an improvement.

The overall result is that conflicts which erupt between established political leaders and their citizens are becoming increasingly violent. More often than not, the side that eventually triumphs rules over a country left in economic ruin.

Ironically, the same electronic technology that makes the peasants more restless also makes the leaders more difficult to unseat. The leaders use electronic devices to learn what the citizens are plotting, and thus we have the age of wiretaps and secret microphones. Recent refinements include the "spike mike," which can be inserted into the wall of an adjoining room, and parabolic microphones, which can pick up conversations from hundreds of feet away. Today a telephone can be turned into a "miketel" capable of intercepting any conversation within hearing range—even without the phone being in use. Even more sophisticated equipment en-

> *In politics we must choose between the strong man whose real interests are elsewhere and who will leave office the moment bigger opportunity beckons, and the weakling who will cling because he can't hold a job anywhere else. Public office is the last refuge of the incompetent.*
>
> —Boise Penrose, 1931

ables a government to intercept any telephone, telegram, or Telex communication transmitted through the air.*

If King George III had had today's electronic equipment, I doubt that America's founding fathers would have succeeded in staging the American Revolution. Today, tyrants are using hundreds of kinds of electronic devices in their efforts to stay in power for life. Thus, unless politically ambitious military leaders stage a coup, or the masses of workers can sustain national strikes for months on end, or a people can be rallied by religious fervor, modern technology gives an edge to the tyrant.

Nuclear Complications

The shortcomings of our leaders, as well as of our inefficient system of choosing them, become magnified when we consider the latest weapons of mass destruction. A few years ago, I was Vice-Chairman of the committee that monitors the laboratories in which America's nuclear weapons are developed. The immense nuclear arsenals

---

*See "A Startling Report on FBI Bugging" by United Press, *San Francisco Chronicle,* May 10, 1976.

possessed by the world powers appalled me. Enormous destructive power is in the hands of the present crop of world politicians, and, in addition to that, some of that power may soon be getting into the hands of even less responsible people.

The blueprint of the atomic bomb is no longer a secret; in the last few years, a number of college students have designed workable bombs. In April 1977, the Congressional Office of Technology Assessment submitted an alarming report to the United States Senate. There is a "clear possibility," it admitted, that even individuals who lack access to classified blueprints could build a nuclear bomb once they got their hands on the nuclear material. It could be done for a fraction of a million dollars. Even now, revolutionaries spend many times that amount on conventional weapons. Again in 1977, the London *Daily Express* reported that one of its employees assembled all the parts of an atomic bomb, except for the plutonium, just to demonstrate how easily terrorists could do it. Upon studying the assemblage and seeing that the bomb was of the same type that the United States had dropped on Hiroshima, a physics professor at London University said: "If I were a member of the government and was shown by a group of terrorists what you have shown me, I would not like to gamble with the lives of thousands of people. I would be terrified."

In a recent issue of *Assassin* magazine that was available at the newsstands, blueprints were given for building an atomic bomb in anyone's basement. The hardware would cost no more than a few thousand dollars.

Even the plans for constructing a hydrogen bomb are no longer known only by a few top government scientists. This is particularly frightening since a hydrogen bomb derives its main energy from the fusion of hydrogen atoms, whereas an atomic bomb requires uranium or plutonium for its energy. Recently, a 36-year-old freelance writer, after studying scientific literature, wrote an article for *Progressive* magazine telling how a hydrogen bomb is made. A federal judge in Madison, Wisconsin, issued an

> *Timid and interested politicians think much
> more about the security of their seats than
> about the security of their country.*
>
> —T. B. Macaulay, 1842

order prohibiting the magazine from publishing the article, because the U.S. Justice Department, after carefully reviewing the
article's contents, rushed to court with documents showing that
"the article provides specific and detailed information concerning
the design and operation of a hydrogen bomb, and technical information necessary to construct such a bomb." The government suit
went on to advise the court that the publication of the information
"would increase proliferation of nuclear weapons, and thereby
severely undercut the arms control and disarmament policies of the
United States."

Now, most of us ignore these facts; what else can we do? We
have to rely on government security surrounding radioactive material and hope that none of it will fall into the hands of terrorists.

Unfortunately, the security surrounding radioactive material throughout the world is often inadequate. With time it will
become even more so. Owing to the rising cost of oil and the need
for power in newly developing nations, nuclear power plants will
continue to be built. In some countries these plants are probably
the nation's only chance to advance from subsistence farming to
industrialization. Over the next decade or so, we will see nuclear
plants being built in some of the remotest countries of the world.
That will mean more nuclear fuel available for bombs—for either
governments or terrorists. India, for example, was quietly obtaining
radioactive material from Canada under the guise of using it as
nuclear fuel for power plants. The world was shocked when India

exploded its own nuclear bomb, thereby joining the nuclear club.

In 1977, the Shah of Iran signed a $9 billion contract with West Germany calling for the eventual construction of four nuclear power plants in addition to the two he already had. Presumably the Shah's downfall will cause West Germany to reconsider its offer. Similarly, France was having some second thoughts recently about its contract to provide a nuclear reprocessing plant for Pakistan. France's President Valery Giscard d'Estaing was apprehensive that Pakistan's military ruler, General Mohammed Zia-ul-Haq, might be tempted to use the plant to produce pure plutonium for use in nuclear weapons.

In December 1977, President Carter threatened to withhold supplies of uranium to South Africa. He wanted South Africa to apply stricter security to prevent its atomic energy program from being used for nuclear weapons. But suppose South Africa, or some developing country, agrees to such conditions. If a coup were to occur—and hardly a month goes by without one occurring somewhere*—who is naive enough to believe that every new leader who seizes power through a coup will abide by a treaty that his predecessor made with an American president? That's probably how nuclear material will ultimately fall into the hands of terrorists.

Now, once a nuclear bomb is detonated in a city the size of Chicago, most of the world's citizens will demand that their leaders use all means to protect society from political terrorists. This demand will virtually guarantee lifetime tenure for existing politicians, because opposition groups will be severely restricted. Thus, if we wait a few more years until terrorists start exploding nuclear weapons, it will be too late to dispassionately seek reforms in the world's political systems.

But even if we forget about terrorists or foreign governments making bombs, the proliferation of nuclear power plants could cause additional problems for the world's political leaders.

---

*See Appendix A.

> *Government has come to be a trade, and is managed solely on commercial principles. A man plunges into politics to make his fortune, and only cares that the world shall last his days.*
>
> —Ralph Waldo Emerson, 1835

One obvious example is the near disaster at Three Mile Island in 1979. Another example which has nothing to do with bombs but just illustrates the size of the problems facing politicians, involves nuclear waste: In 1977, a commercial reprocessing plant in New York state went out of business. Later, to ensure that the necessary safeguards to protect the environment had been taken, a congressional committee investigated the site. The congressmen were shocked to learn that $632 million was needed to dispose of the waste material left around the abandoned plant. At the site, 612,-000 gallons of liquid waste and 2,100,000 cubic feet of solid waste had to be removed, to ensure that the waste would not endanger future generations. Now ask yourself what would happen in a newly emerging country after it has had its nuclear plants in operation for a few years. Then, because of economic pressures, perhaps famine, the government is overthrown and its nuclear plants sabotaged and rendered inoperative. If it costs in excess of $600 million to safeguard one defunct nuclear reprocessing plant in the U.S., where can any small country suffering from economic chaos find even a fraction of that amount of money? It's unreasonable to assume that hungry masses would permit their government to divert that kind of money from food in order to build concrete coffins for radioactive mud that to the naked eye and touch appears perfectly harmless.

Problems like these are too big for the kinds of politicians the world has today; such problems call for solutions from the wisest among us. It is not political systems that have failed. Perhaps, they

all could work well for their particular societies. It is the leaders
who make the systems fail. The hundreds of pressing problems with
which the political leaders of the world must deal are of such magnitude and urgency that any one of the problems could alone legiti-
mately lay claim to the leaders' complete interest for their every
waking moment. But, unfortunately for the world, none of those
problems can even rate better than second place to something else
with which the politicians' attention is more fully occupied—
namely, the perpetuation of themselves in political office.

"Let 'em try their reforms . . . we'll bury 'em with a Xerox barrage in quintuplicate"

5 | Earlier Remedies

Before the world was organized into nations, the human race was divided into much smaller groups such as tribes, villages, and city-states. Thus, thousands of schemes for government must have been devised over the centuries. Many of these groups, from the most primitive to the most advanced, sought to restrain their leaders. Before discussing some attempts at restraint in the United States, it may be interesting to consider a few examples from other lands.

Nontechnological Societies

According to legend, rulers in ancient India were required to resign after twelve years in power, give away all their worldly goods—both their own and their family's—and become one with the poor, never to rule again. Under such a system it is very likely that a leader will be extremely concerned with improving the lot of those whom he will eventually join.

In ancient Greece, we find that the Athenians chose their new archon, or chief executive, every year. This system of extremely short political terms must have been responsible to some degree for the citizens' feelings of individual freedom and for the setting in which flourished one of the highest civilizations in world history.

In modern India, the Totas tribe has no formal leaders whatsoever. If a dispute arises, a committee of elders convenes to deal with it. Once the problem is resolved, the committee disbands.

A tribe in contemporary Africa has devised an equally unusual approach to leadership. Once a year, the leader must walk blindfolded between two rows made up of all the men in the tribe. The chief is then hit with a stick by everyone as hard or as softly as each man wishes. The knowledge that a disgruntled tribesman might fracture his skull must certainly keep the people's welfare uppermost in the chief's mind throughout the rest of the year.

Appealing as it may be to some, the custom of annually impoverishing, dismissing, or cudgeling our leaders will not work in modern society. But we must devise some way to control the politicians. While in this chapter I will focus on American attempts to limit political tenure, I would like to stress that the need for limited tenure exists in every nation of the world.

The United States

In the United States, public opinion has recently begun to favor limited terms of office. In March 1978, Senator Malcolm Wallop (Rep., Wyoming) made this statement to a congressional hearing on tenure: "A recent Gallup poll indicates that 60 percent of the eligible American voters favor some law limiting senators and representatives to a maximum of twelve years in office." He then went on to say: "A similar Gallup poll reveals that senators and congressmen rate relatively low on a list of twenty occupations in terms of both honesty and ethical standards. Could this mistrust of Senate and House of Representatives arise because we no longer perceive ourselves as citizen legislators?"

At that same hearing, Senator John C. Danforth (Rep., Missouri), commenting on that recent Gallup study, said: "People across the country have lost faith in their government."

George Gallup himself, commenting on the proposal to limit congressional tenure, stated: "There are those who argue that it might deprive the nation of the services of individuals of extraordinary talent, and government is so complex that years are required for a legislator to familiarize himself with it. But room would also be made for individuals of equal, or greater, talent, who might otherwise never get to Congress" ("Six Political Reforms Most Americans Want," *Reader's Digest,* August 1978, p. 60).

In the Beginning . . .

During the past 190 years, most members of Congress have failed to see the need for limiting congressional careers. Nevertheless, there have been a few voices from time to time who did advocate some limitation. Not surprisingly, their proposals received little support. The first such proposal for a Constitutional Amendment, presented to Congress in 1789, would have limited service in the House to six years in any eight-year period. It was rejected, perhaps because few members at that time ever intended to stay in Congress for more than six years.

Indeed, when the country first started, the framers of the Constitution did not even envision congressional service as a full-time occupation. In those days, Congress only convened for less than four months every year. The congressmen, who were the leading citizens of their communities, would return home to their normal occupations for the remaining eight months. Furthermore, few of them ever thought of serving more than two two-year terms, for a total tenure of four years. What is particularly interesting about all this is that even though one might have been a congressman for four years, he would not have been in the nation's capital for more than a total of one year and four months.

This tradition of members of the House generally serving only two terms and then returning home to their previous occupations continued up until 1869. Unfortunately, from the Civil War up to the 1920s, the tradition died. The average length of congressional tenure then doubled, going from four years to eight.

Another way of looking at this situation is to consider that back in the nineteenth century about 45 percent of the congressional seats changed hands in every election. In the twentieth cen-

> *Politics are now nothing more than means of rising in the world.*
>
> —Samuel Johnson, 1775

tury, however, most incumbents are returned to office. In fact, since World War II, almost 93 percent of the politicians seeking reelection have succeeded.*

These figures certainly do not mean that our leaders do such an outstanding job that we are reluctant to replace them. Rather, as many observers have noted, congressional longevity is linked to the inventions of radio and television. In the previous chapter, I mentioned how the income tax laws have given Congress increasingly greater funds and therefore unprecedented power. Because those in Congress are now in fact so powerful and so important, the news media keep them constantly before the public. Because of news coverage, it is easier for incumbents to build their public images and collect campaign funds. Unknown contenders, on the other hand, are at a tremendous disadvantage in trying to defeat these political celebrities. Consequently, some limitation is necessary.

The 22nd Amendment

In 1951, the 22nd Amendment to the Constitution placed a two-term limitation on the presidency. That was the first successful step in limiting political tenure. It was a long time in coming, although many previous Presidents had urged such a limitation.

---

*Testimony of John C. Gartland, Director, Foundation for the Study of Presidential and Congressional Terms, Senate Subcommittee Hearing, March 16, 1978.

In 1809, for example, Thomas Jefferson wrote: "I prefer the presidential term of four years, . . . annexing to it, however, ineligibility forever after. . . ."

In 1834, Andrew Jackson suggested that the President serve for a "single period of either four or six years."

James Polk, Andrew Johnson, and Rutherford B. Hayes all went on record in favor of one term.

In 1884, Grover Cleveland expressed his preference for a single term. The possibility of reelection, he wrote, posed a danger "to that calm, deliberate, and intelligent political action which must characterize a government by the people."

Ex-President William Howard Taft pointed out in 1915 that a single term would "give the executive greater courage and independence in the discharge of his duties."

An Amendment for Congress

In 1951, after the passage of the 22nd Amendment, President Truman proposed a limit of twelve years of service in each chamber of Congress, and his proposal received heated debate. As one might suspect, some congressmen who had enthusiastically supported the 22nd Amendment viewed President Truman's proposal as a threat to themselves. It did not pass.

Another series of attempts was made in the late 1950s and early 1960s by Congressman Thomas B. Curtis (Rep., Missouri). Curtis proposed an amendment to the Constitution limiting all members of both houses to twelve consecutive years in office, at the end of which a two-year "sabbatical" was required before one could run again. It, too, did not pass.

While the Curtis amendment did not become law, President Truman was not the only President in favor of it. In 1963, former President Eisenhower supported Curtis's proposal. "What is good for the President," he said, "may very well be good for Congress."

> *Ignorance, idleness and vice may be
> sometimes the only ingredients for qualifying
> a legislator.*
>
> —Jonathan Swift, 1726

Eisenhower added that, under this amendment, each congressman "would tend to think of his congressional career as an important and exciting interlude in his life, a period dedicated to the entire public rather than a way of making a living. The members would probably give more attention to national good and less to their political fortunes."

Even President Kennedy, referring to the Curtis amendment, said: "It's the sort of proposal I may advance in a post-presidential period...."

While the recommendations of Presidents Truman and Eisenhower were rejected, the idea has become increasingly popular. From 1929 to 1971, there were fifteen resolutions calling for a restricted congressional tenure—that is, about one resolution in Congress every three years. But now the need for such a limitation has become so urgent that fourteen resolutions proposing limited terms were introduced in Congress in 1977 alone.

Such amendments are even being proposed at the state level. In California, a recently introduced bill would have placed a twelve-year limitation on consecutive service in any one political office. Had the bill passed, politicians would have been required to take a two-year leave every twelve years.

Several major reasons underlie this recent clamoring. To begin with, most of the public is thoroughly dissatisfied with Congress. Many critics, myself included, feel that the unchecked power of the federal government has become oppressive. And the unrestrained bureaucracies which Congress created, perhaps with good intentions, are running wild.

Our present system of representation is not a healthy one. Incumbents tend to move into Washington and send their children to school there. After several years in office, Washington becomes their "hometown." Numerous observers, including Senator John C. Danforth, wonder "if being a Washington type is the kind of experience a person really should have. There is at least as much wisdom spread throughout the country as there is here," he said. "I am one who does not believe that Washington has some monopoly on intelligence or on the right kind of experience."

The intense pace of Washington politics takes its toll. Representative Toby Moffett (Dem., Connecticut) said in 1978: "I think what happens is not that we don't have good people, but that most of us are subjected to a process which wears us down, which erodes principles, which tires out people, and which takes away our sense of urgency, and our sense of outrage. That happens to the best of people in the institution."

Senator Harrison H. Schmitt (Rep., New Mexico) agreed with Moffett. "My experience in other endeavors," he said, "has shown me that ten or twelve years of intense activity are about the limit that most individuals find they can maintain before they start to feel a little stale and become less effective than they were at the height of their powers. A change in career rejuvenates and again produces a person capable of contributing to the maximum of his capability."

Senator Dennis DeConcini (Dem., Arizona) asserted in 1978 that "by shortening terms, I feel that legislative accountability will be enhanced."

The task of a true statesman is to vote for what is best for the nation and to inform his constituents why he so voted. Unfortunately, when there are no limitations on terms of office, statesmanship is difficult to find. The human tendency to preserve oneself in ego-gratifying high political office is overwhelming. The tempta-

> *Politics is perhaps the only profession for which no preparation is thought necessary.*
>
> —Robert Louis Stevenson, 1882

tion is to say yes to everybody, no to nobody, and hope that everyone votes for you at the next election. Now, what kind of government is that?

Consciously or unconsciously, career legislators resist changes that threaten their jobs. It is usually the recently arrived congressmen who acknowledge the need for limited tenure, but they are in the minority. So if we wait for the majority of politicians to reform the political system, our prospects are bleak.

In the past few years, thirty-two congressmen have proposed legislation to limit congressional tenure. One such proposal (Senate Joint Resolution 28, dated February 24, 1977), authored by Senators Danforth, DeConcini, Goldwater, Schmitt, Wallop, and Hayakawa, would place a twelve-year limit on congressional terms. While this is a step in the right direction, I don't think the resolution goes far enough. Under it a politician could still go from unlimited years in city, county, or state government to twelve years in the House and then twelve more years in the Senate. In other words, a shrewd politician could still spend a lifetime in politics.

While no politician actually uses the term "demagogue's disease," some nevertheless understand the concept perfectly well. Representative Berkley Bedell (Dem., Iowa) used the term "Washingtonitis" to refer to "a serious danger of growing stale in Washington." "It is," he said, "a *disease* which, in varying degrees, affects all members of Congress."

"All too often," said Senator S. I. Hayakawa (Rep., California) in 1978, "we forget that we are farmers, teachers, and businessmen, not Greek gods." In the same year, another legislator, who preferred to remain anonymous, said: "Let's face it, a lot of us are on a real ego trip."

In 1977, as Senator DeConcini delicately urged support for the congressional tenure limitation amendment that he had co-sponsored, ninety of his colleagues were accused of accepting bribes from the government of South Korea. It must have been difficult for the senator to keep a smile from creeping over his face as he said: "I am loath to quote Lord Acton's dictum about the corrupting nature of power because I do not believe that any Member of this Chamber or of the House of Representatives has been corrupted by power. It is the possibility that exists: and it is that possibility that we must guard against." Perhaps if Senator DeConcini could have spoken as a non-politician, he would have said: "Look, all of us who have the privilege of sitting in these historic chambers have the demagogue's disease—and we all know it! And each year we remain in office the disease worsens, and by continually running for reelection we do a disservice to our states and the nation."

In his *Autobiography,* published in 1929, the usually laconic Calvin Coolidge had a lot to say on this subject:

> It is difficult for men in high office to avoid the malady of self-delusion. They are always surrounded by worshippers. They are constantly and for the most part sincerely assured of their greatness.
>
> They live in an artificial atmosphere of adulation and exaltation which sooner or later impairs their judgment. They are in grave danger of becoming careless and arrogant.
>
> The chances of having wise and faithful public service are increased by a change in the presidential office after a moderate length of time.

Obviously, change is needed. As we have seen, from Thomas Jefferson on down, some of our greatest leaders have advocated it. The question is, will the politicians ever vote for it?

"I have always been an advocate of weeding the incompetents out of government service as long as it doesn't affect the elected ones!"

6 | Cure

Bandages on the Disease

None of the proposals made in recent years to cure our political ills are adequate, because none of them go far enough. They certainly won't rid us of career politicians, and some of the proposals might even make the situation worse.

Consider the proposal which would limit service in either house of the U.S. Congress to twelve years. It overlooks the fact that instead of political newcomers entering Congress, there will be a horde of career politicians who have already spent fifteen or twenty years in state legislatures now scrambling for those federal seats. In fact, under such a proposal, the politicians who finally get to Congress are going to be scheming and campaigning for the next change of office even more than they do now, because they won't be able to stay in the House or the Senate for more than twelve years each, but nothing will prevent them from running for office in the other house of Congress or at some other elective level in their states.

While such proposals may be made with good intentions, I feel that they are no more than bandages on the disease. Such proposals cannot halt the worldwide trends that are destroying the political freedom that the human race has been struggling for centuries to achieve. If these trends are allowed to continue, dictatorship will become the sole form of government throughout the world. Not because people are unprepared for democracy, but because the politicians of the world, by their very conduct, will prevent democracy from succeeding.

Democracy, whereby leaders are chosen by the people, is a great idea. It has flaws and inefficiencies, but it can work well if only given a chance. Unfortunately, professional vote-seekers who devise ingenious, often unscrupulous ways to remain in high office are unintentionally sabotaging democracy.

But democracy doesn't have to fail. If we make a slight adjustment in its selection system, we will be surprised how well democracy can work.

The need to limit political tenure is not restricted to democracy, however; it is applicable to any system in the world enfeebled by the demagogue's disease. A glance at history will show that leaders addicted to power and glory have flourished under feudalism, capitalism, fascism, socialism, communism, and every other kind of political *ism*.

A Total Cure

The adjustment I seek goes beyond limiting the number of years that a politician can serve in any one particular office. Instead, it limits the *total* number of years that a politician can be active in elective politics at any and all levels.

Under such an adjustment, a nation would start limiting leaders to say, four or six years in office—the exact number would be decided by each nation. This rapid turnover, sending leaders back home to live under laws they helped to enact, will bring many improvements. First of all, the leaders will be fully aware that politics is not a lifelong career, and thus their wisdom is not likely to be diminished by future political ambitions. In other words, the leaders of the world will leave politics for good before the demagogue's disease has had a chance to envelop them.

We must also keep in mind that with tenure limitation we are going to draw our leaders from an entirely different pool of talent. Today, mediocre career politicians claw their way to their level of incompetence and struggle to remain there. Tomorrow, citizen politicians, after contributing a few years of their lives to their country, will return to their former careers. These new leaders will appeal to our highest ideals, not our lowest instincts.

A Global Village

But suppose that a country changes its constitution and sets a limit on political tenure, and then the leader of that country tries to violate the limit in his nation's constitution. What then? Once the world recognizes the chaos that is created when politicians stay in office too long, the people in other countries, out of self-interest, will want to stop it. Therefore, political and economic sanctions from the international community should be the response.

Since the world is a global village, to use McLuhan's apt phrase, any steps we take to improve its leadership will create benefits that will flow from individuals, to nations, to humanity in general.

One immediate benefit to the world at large would be decreased military spending. As Ruth L. Sivard reports in *World Military and Social Expenditures* (available from the World Without War Council, 1730 Grove St., Berkeley, California, 94703), military expenditures on a worldwide scale will amount to over $3 trillion in the 1970s alone. If only a small portion of that sum were diverted, we could feed, educate, and provide proper medical care for the underprivileged children throughout the world. The pathetic little beggar girl I met in the village in Southeast Asia and children like her everywhere would no longer have to exist in such poverty.

With more resources available for the common good, the entire world would benefit and there would be less discontent. That, in turn, could eventually produce further reductions in military expenses, with fewer armored divisions poised at national borders. Thus, the world would become a less threatening place, and the chances of a nuclear war would be reduced.

> *One of the principal qualifications for a
> political job is that the applicant know
> nothing much about what he is expected to
> do.*
>
> —Terry M. Townsend, 1940

Another benefit would be that higher education would be fully encouraged all over the world, for leaders would no longer fear educated citizens; and schools, which are now ordered closed in so many countries when students protest a leader's excesses, would remain open.

Politicians, elected for competence rather than for their abilities as performers, would concern themselves less with public relations and more with the problems of their nations. With little need to further their political careers, they would have ample time to concentrate on issues and less need to avoid problems by creating autonomous bureaucracies. They would find it easier to say no to every special interest group, and they could offer statesmanlike solutions to the world's pressing problems, thus truly promoting human advancement. The fact is that there is no end to the amount of good that one can accomplish in this world if he is not concerned with who gets the credit for it.

The new kind of leader would not be likely to equate national security with his remaining in office. Claims such as Hitler's inflated boast that his Reich would endure for a thousand years would have a hollow ring, and the pathological personality would be discouraged, if not barred, from entering politics in the first place.

Such simple adjustments in political selection can arrest the demagogue's disease and help the world—both to survive and to become a better place.

A Hopeful Analogy

As I indicated earlier, smallpox once ravaged the planet, and mankind was helpless to do anything about it. Today, thanks to a simple solution, the principle of immunization, smallpox is a thing of the past.

But the remedy for smallpox was not adopted all at once. In fact, people from various walks of life, including writers and cartoonists, ridiculed the idea at first. However, after a handful of people were inoculated and thereby spared the agony of the disease, others accepted the treatment. Eventually, smallpox vaccination became so universally accepted that each country placed guards at its borders to turn back anyone who had *not* been vaccinated.

Likewise, my idea of limiting the number of years that a person will be allowed to engage in politics may be ridiculed in the beginning. However, sooner or later some countries will try it. Under that new leadership, those nations will become so successful that all nations will eventually resort to the same cure.

Given the rapid rate of change in the world, I wouldn't be surprised if limited political tenure is accepted more or less universally within a generation. But this remedy for the demagogue's disease is available to all of us today. When the people choose to administer it, the gross ineffectiveness of government will end, and the need for violent coups and revolutions will vanish. At that point, we will have freed ourselves from a political disease that for too long has plagued us all.

The Story in Pictures

How sweet it is!

UPI Photo

President Nixon acknowledging the enthusiastic response of the people of Savannah, Georgia, October 14, 1970.

How sweet it was!

President Nixon as he boards a helicopter on the White House lawn shortly after resigning from office. Washington, D.C., August 9, 1974.

It is a very ego-inflating experience to be an important politician. Wherever one goes, there are admirers wishing to take his picture or touch his hand or the hem of his garment. Notice the mother lifting her son's arm in the hope that his hand will come in contact with the great man. It is very human of us to pay our respects in this manner, but the recipient of the adulation also has human feelings, and it is a rare individual who does not succumb to an exaggerated sense of self-importance. In fact, in this human desire to touch one's hero, the demagogue's disease is transmitted to the leader almost as if it were literally a germ on the hands of the worshipers.

UPI Photo

President Nixon greeting tourists in the Capitol Plaza, Washington, D.C., May 11, 1971.

As one becomes more exalted in his political rank, the admiring public prevents him from leading a normal private life. Even when he occasionally goes out to enjoy a ball game, he is the center of attraction. If he refuses to play this role in a democracy, the people will not reelect him. No one event is harmful in itself, but a career of such admiration is unhealthy for the politician and the nation.

UPI Photo

President Nixon winding up to throw out the first ball in Anaheim, California, as the American League opens its 1973 baseball season, April 6, 1973.

When the leader acquires the habit of looking down at his
people from great heights, he can hardly distinguish their
faces and almost certainly will have difficulty seeing and
understanding their problems.

UPI Photo

Chilean military junta leader General Augusto Pinochet and his wife looking down on the largest public demonstration of support ever seen in
Chile, an estimated 750,000 people in Santiago cheering the first anniversary of the military coup that ousted the government of Salvador Allende.
September 11, 1974.

UPI Photo

Generalissimo Francisco Franco extending his hands over an enormous crowd in Madrid, Spain. October 1970.

Much as the Caesars triumphantly entered Rome, the present-day politician experiences and savors the exhilarating parades in his honor, passing thousands of waving and cheering supporters. Are humans emotionally equipped for a life career that has such perquisites, and still retain common sense and wisdom? Even the Caesars had their whispering slaves to remind them that they were mortal.

President Nixon and Egyptian President Anwar Sadat riding in triumph through Alexandria, Egypt, on June 13, 1974. Two months later, Nixon will resign from office.

Sheikh Mujibur Rahman (center on truck) being greeted by more than half a million of his followers on January 10, 1972, as he returns to Dacca, Bangladesh, to become the Prime Minister, after nine months of imprisonment in Pakistan. It will not be long before he enacts laws allowing warrantless arrests, the banning of public meetings, and unlimited detention of government opponents, including Maulana Bhashani, the 90-year-old opposition leader. In August 1975, he will be assassinated in a military coup.

One typical sign that a leader has the demagogue's disease appears when he starts having statues of himself erected throughout the country. Wisdom is a very frail substance: it can hardly survive in the limelight, and perishes almost at once when placed on a pedestal.

UPI Photo

President Idi Amin Dada unveiling a statue of himself in Kampala, Uganda, July 24, 1975.

A common occurrence in this electronic age of ours is the array of microphones thrust in front of politicians, signifying that the world awaits their every utterance. How long could you or I be treated like this without our humility being affected?

UPI Photo

President Nikolai Podgorny of the Soviet Union in Paris, France, for the memorial service of President Charles de Gaulle, November 13, 1970.

At a time when the world most desperately needs wisdom in
leadership, our science and technology— through television—
make the selection of leaders turn more on acting ability and
beauty.

Wide World Photo

Mrs. Cornelia Wallace shows George's "bad side" during the presidential
primary campaign in Florida, January 27, 1972.

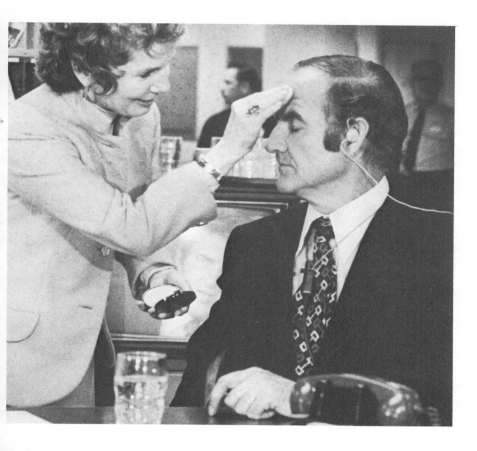

Senator George McGovern being prepared by his wife for a TV interview in the newsroom of the *Milwaukee Journal,* Milwaukee, Wisconsin, April 4, 1972.

The demagogue's disease often evolves from the people's need to worship heroes.

UPI Photo

A third of a million union members marching for Juan and Isabel Peron in Buenos Aires, Argentina, September 7, 1973. Peron had returned to Argentina three months earlier, following eighteen years in exile.

Chinese workers marching in a National Day parade, October 1, 1950.

Even the diplomatic courtesies and honors given by other countries make politicians feel important.

UPI Photo

President Jean Bedel Bokassa of the Central African Republic being escorted by French President Charles de Gaulle to the Champs-sur-Marie Castle, where Bokassa will stay as a guest of France. February 11, 1969.

Princess Margaret of Great Britain curtsies to the Shah of Iran on his arrival at Victoria Station, London, May 5, 1959. Looking on are Queen Elizabeth II (in white) and Prince Philip (with his back to the camera) (right).

Paris Mayor Jacques Chirac welcoming Soviet President Leonid Brezhnev to the Paris City Hall for a reception given in his honor. June 21, 1977.

Generalissimo Francisco Franco (center) reviewing the annual military parade marking his victory in the Spanish Civil War. Behind him is his designated successor, Prince Juan Carlos. Madrid, Spain, May 31, 1970.

Another heady experience, and one that may tend over the years to dehumanize a chief of state, is the reviewing of military might.

Saudi Arabia's King Faisal (left) and Jordan's King Hussein reviewing Jordanian troops in Amman, Jordan, February 2, 1966. Nine years later, King Faisal will be assassinated and buried in an unmarked grave.

Congolese President Joseph Kasavubu (center) saluting as he walks past Tunisian UN troops in Leopoldville, Congo, June 2, 1961. To the left (also saluting) is General Joseph Mobutu, who will lead a successful military coup to overthrow Kasavubu in 1965, and who will himself be overthrown by yet another military coup in 1968 (below, left).

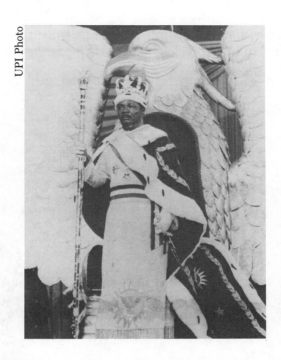

Emperor Jean Bedel Bokassa of the Central African Empire, wearing a crown studded with 2,000 diamonds, stands in front of his two-ton throne crafted in the shape of a giant gilded eagle. December 4, 1977.

When national leaders engage in excessive self-adornment, it is a clear warning that the country is in trouble.

His dress uniform ablaze with medals, Uganda's President Idi Amin Dada attends a meeting of the Organization of African Unity in Libreville, Gabon, July 2, 1977. President Amin came to power through a coup six years earlier and, after a number of attempts by the military to overthrow him, was driven from power by an army of exiles in April 1979. (Above.)

Standing smartly at attention in Baghdad, Iraq, are (left to right) Iraqi Deputy Premier and Defense Minister, Lieutenant General Hardan Takriti, President Hamed Hassan Al-Bakr, and Chief of Staff, Lieutenant General Hamad Chehab. July 24, 1969. President Al-Bakr came to power through a coup the year before (left.)

Is it a sign of the madness of power, or as the French call it, *folie de grandeur,* to imitate Napoleon by crowning oneself emperor and one's wife empress?

The Shah of Iran crowning his wife Empress Farah, moments after crowning himself. Looking on is their seven-year-old son, Crown Prince Riza. This is the first time in the entire history of Iran that a crown sits on the head of a woman. November 1, 1967.

UPI Photo

After crowning himself, Emperor Jean Bedel Bokassa of the Central African Empire crowns his wife Catherine. The lavish and spectacular coronation ceremony cost his impoverished nation one-fourth of its annual earnings from all exports. In the foreground is Bokassa's heir designate, two-year-old Jean Bedel Jr. December 4, 1977. A year later, there will be reports of a "reign of terror" in which the imperial guard bayonet and club to death dozens of children for being disrespectful toward the emperor.

UPI Photo

On January 27, 1970, President Nixon revealed a new gold-braided, European look with Prussian-style helmets for the White House guards. Within a month, the public denunciation of the new garb was such that the uniforms had to be considerably toned down.

Presidents who can't see the way to declare themselves king or emperor can dress up their guards to make the executive mansion look like a palace.

"Whoever exalts himself will be humbled."
—Matthew 23:12

Il Duce ("The Leader") Benito Mussolini appears before the people of Milan on November 9, 1936.

But the demagogue's disease is not limited to only the most ruthless of rulers. Today's victim can become tomorrow's demagogue.

Emperor Haile Selassie, once the chief victim of Mussolini's aggression, receives Giovanni Brusasca, the Italian Under-Secretary of Foreign Affairs, in Addis Ababa, Ethiopia, September 14, 1951. Twenty-three years later, after ruling his country with an iron fist for fifty-three years, the Emperor was deposed by a military coup in 1974, and later died while under house arrest. The new leaders of Ethiopia have successfully wiped out all traces of him.

Il Duce (left) appears before the people of Milan with his mistress, Clara Petacci, and Lieutenant General Achille Starace (right) on April 30, 1945 (below, left).

Yesterday's demagogue can also become today's victim.

A statue of the Shah of Iran's father, Reza Shah, being pulled down by demonstrators in Tehran moments after Shah Mohammed Reza Pahlavi left Iran on January 16, 1979.

"My advisers built a wall between myself and my people. I didn't realize what was happening. When I woke up, I had lost my people."

—Shah of Iran

An Iranian soldier kisses the feet of Shah Mohammed Reza Pahlavi as aides of the monarch look on grimly and Empress Farah looks away with a big smile just minutes before the Shah flees the country. Tehran, January 16, 1979.

If a leader has ambitions to stay in power for a long time, he
usually concludes that it is more important to keep the military happy than the citizens.

The Chilean military junta listens as President Augusto Pinochet addresses
the nation via radio and television on the second anniversary of the coup
that ousted the regime of Salvador Allende. Santiago, September 12, 1975.

Moroccan Defense Minister General Mohamed Oufkir kissing the hand of King Hassan II in 1966. Six years later the general will try to overthrow the King, and when the attempted coup fails he will put a bullet through his own head.

Instead of being ruled by military men, would a country be better off under the care of a physician? Here is one who resolved to try to put an end to the tyranny and oppression of his nation's poor people. It was not long, however, before he came to love the luxuries of palace life, and, with a fully developed case of the demagogue's disease, he resorted to some of the cruelest and most diabolical tortures to keep the peasants from agitating for his removal from office.

Heavily armed soldiers surround President François "Papa Doc" Duvalier (wearing glasses) in Port-au-Prince, Haiti, May 13, 1963. A year later he had himself declared President-for-life.

It is characteristic of the demagogue's disease that once one gets into power he soon suffers from delusions of grandeur and wants to establish a dynasty. Here is a twenty-year-old president-for-life who was willed absolute power over his people by the former president-for-life, his father.

Jean-Claude "Baby Doc" Duvalier reviewing army troops under the armed escort of General Gracia Jacques, who is carrying a submachine gun and an automatic pistol and appears to be ready for any emergency. Port-au-Prince, Haiti, April 26, 1971.

If a doctor is susceptible to the demagogue's disease, perhaps a religious leader would be immune?

Archbishop Makarios, for eighteen years President of Cyprus, quieting a woman in a Greek Orthodox church in London. Makarios, who died two months later, was in London to attend a conference. December 14, 1977.

The Ayatollah Ruhollah Khomeini and his followers praying for the fall of the Shah of Iran. Weeks later their prayers were answered. Neauphle, Le Chateau, France, December 7, 1978.

If men contract the demagogue's disease when in high office too long, why not choose women as leaders? May they not be immune to the disease of power and glory?

UPI Photo

Mrs. Sirimavo Bandaranaike, Prime Minister of Sri Lanka (Ceylon), assuming a prayerful posture at a Buddhist temple in London, March 6, 1961. Ten years later, during an anti-government uprising, Mrs. Bandaranaike presided over the execution of 15,000 people, most of them youths. Some victims were made to dig their own graves and were lined up and shot, while others were hung by their feet and tortured. These atrocities were committed openly in order to terrorize the population. Mrs. Bandaranaike was finally defeated in the general elections of 1977, in which the major issues were nepotism, abuses of power, and corruption, in addition to the poor economic situation.

One of the most obvious signs of the demagogue's disease is the politician's inclination to find leadership ability among members of his own immediate family.

UPI Photo

When the state constitution of Alabama prohibited Governor George Wallace from serving another term in office, he had his wife Lurleen run for the job. Here, he looks over her shoulder in the state capitol as she affixes her signature to an official document. Montgomery, Alabama, March 16, 1967.

Argentina's President Juan Peron and his wife, Vice–President Isabel Peron, waving to their enthusiastic supporters from the balcony of Government House in Buenos Aires, June 12, 1974.

Seventeen days later, on June 29, 1974, Isabel Peron speaks on national radio and television in Buenos Aires to announce that she has assumed the presidency because her husband is too ill to carry on. Less than two years later, on March 24, 1976, this first woman chief of state in the Americas will be deposed by the military and placed under house arrest.

Even the nonpolitical spouses of high-ranking political leaders may succumb to the demagogue's disease.

Mrs. Abraham Lincoln appearing in one of her lavish banquet gowns. She took the position that as First Lady it was her duty to be better dressed and more elegant than any other woman in the nation. Like many queens of Europe, she purchased far more dresses and yard goods than she could ever possibly use, and in the process she put her husband deep into debt.

It has been said that the only thing we learn from history is that we never learn from history. What country is there, whether capitalist, communist, or third world, that has not put its trust in a young dynamic leader, only to find that, years later, no matter how old or ill he may be, that same leader mistakenly believes that only he can solve the problems of his country? When any leader anywhere in the world keeps himself in power too long, his nation will eventually suffer and the subsequent generations of his people will condemn his lack of wisdom in not retiring from power earlier to permit others to assist in his country's progress.

UPI Photo

Generalissimo and Madame Chiang Kai-shek celebrating the return of the Nationalist government to Nanking, China, May 5, 1946. They have just paid their respects at the tomb of Sun Yat-sen, founder of the Chinese Republic. Would Sun Yat-sen, who devoted his entire life to abolishing the very concept of dynasty, have wanted his disciple to remain in office into his late eighties and then pass on his authority to his own son Chiang Ching-kuo?

UPI Photo

Chairman Mao's wife, Chiang Ch'ing (center), with Premier Chou En-lai (left), receiving the warm applause and greetings of the throng in Peking's Tienanmen Square, May 1, 1973. Four years later, many of these same citizens will condemn Chiang Ch'ing as one of the hated "Gang of Four" and concede that Mao himself stayed in power too long.

More than half of the people of the world today are being ruled by leaders in their seventies and eighties, many of them suffering from illnesses that reduce their mental and physical abilities, or both. On the mental side, it is not just senility that should give us concern. The fact is that humans start to lose their wisdom the longer they are in high positions of power and glory.

UPI Photo

Spain's 80-year-old Generalissimo Francisco Franco greeting his cabinet members. Behind Franco is his designated successor, 35-year-old Prince Juan Carlos. Madrid, Spain, 1973.

UPI Photo

China's Mao Tse-tung, at age 82, meeting with Pakistan's Prime Minister Zulfikar Ali Bhutto (right) in Peking, May 27, 1976. Within three years, Ali Bhutto will be overthrown by a military coup, convicted of killing a rival, and executed by hanging.

One of the problems plaguing the world today is the fact that through medical science the lives of politicians are able to be prolonged much beyond the norms experienced in any other century. Thus, we are not only stuck with power-hungry leaders, but we have to put up with them until they die from either old age or a bullet.

UPI Photo

The $14 million yacht Al Riadh (above), as it appeared upon its completion in an Amsterdam shipyard on Jaunary 20, 1978. The yacht is about to sail with its 22-man crew to Saudi Arabia, where it will serve at the pleasure of its owner, King Khaled. To be on the safe side, the king had his yacht outfitted with the most up-to-date medical equipment, a small part of which is seen here (right).

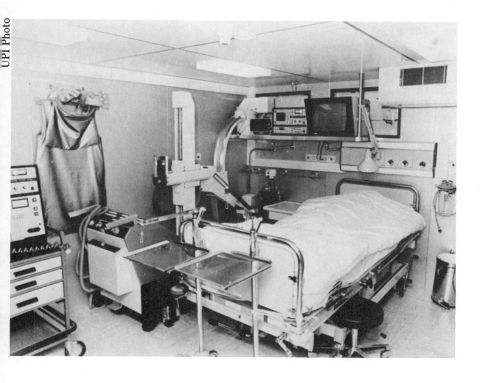

Great Britain long ago realized the evil of concentrating both
the power and the glory of government in one ruler. Accordingly, under the British system, the glory of high office resides
with the crown while the real power to govern the country is
executed by the Prime Minister and Parliament. Must the
newly emerging nations go through generations of agony and
suffering before they, too, realize the danger of permitting too
much power to be concentrated in too few hands?

Prince Philip, Duke of Edinburgh, listens as Queen
Elizabeth II opens Parliament by reading the Labour
Government's plans for the British economy. Novem-
ber 1, 1978.

No matter how small or insignificant a country may be, its leaders continually demonstrate that military might is the answer to the world's problems.

Colonel Moammar Khadafy of Libya (with arms crossed) shopping for the latest in military hardware in Belgrade, Yugoslavia, January 27, 1974.

As political leaders continually stress the importance of military weapons for the solution of political problems, the younger generations come to believe that, indeed, all power comes from the barrel of a gun.

A Cambodian boy loads an M-16 rifle for his father during a battle eighteen miles southeast of Phnom Penh, November 18, 1974.

Children at Camilo Cienfuegos Pioneer Camp in Havana, Cuba, practicing how to dismantle and reassemble a Soviet-made AK-47 automatic rifle even with a blindfold on. February 16, 1977.

A young Christian militiaman brandishing his Soviet-made AK-47 automatic rifle in Beirut, Lebanon, September 9, 1978.

A typical scene today in most of the countries of Africa, Asia, and South and Central America: soldiers going forth to kill and die in order to bring about some "change of government" which will simply mean that an old demagogue is replaced by a new one.

Soldiers of the Popular Movement for the Liberation of Angola moving up to front lines to fight forces of the National Front for the Liberation of Angola. Caxito, Angola, December 19, 1975.

American tanks, West Berlin, May 14, 1977.

Soviet tanks, Red Square, Moscow, November 7, 1977.

UPI Photo

East German missiles, East Berlin, October 7, 1977.

"Every gun that is made, every warship launched, every rocket fired signifies, in the final sense, a theft from those who hunger and are not fed, those who are cold and are not clothed."

—President Dwight D. Eisenhower

While the politicians of the world play their power games, helpless children are suffering and dying from the crippling effects of malnutrition. Often the needed food supplies are rotting in the country's warehouses while the children suffer irreparable damage to mind and body because of bureaucratic blundering, inefficiency, or corruption.

UPI Photo

Suffering from dehydration, a child is too weak to move at a refugee camp in drought-stricken Somalia. April 17, 1975.

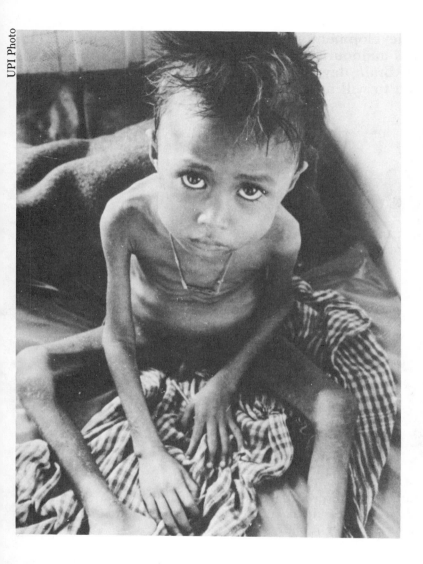

UPI Photo

Of all the children with only a matter of time to die at a pediatric ward in Phnom Penh, Cambodia, this boy is the only one who can manage to sit up. The hospital came to be known as "the place they take children to die." March 15, 1975.

"Brain development cannot take place in the fetus if the mother is malnourished, nor can it take place if the infant is starving. Brain development that does not occur when it is supposed to will never take place."

—Meals for Millions

UPI Photo

A destitute victim of drought, this little Indian boy already blinded by malnutrition waits beside his mother while his food ration for a week is weighed out. October 7, 1967.

UPI Photo

A volunteer worker feeds one of 500 children housed in a disused maternity home in Port Harcourt, Nigeria, January 21, 1970. The children were brought here from the former Biafran Enclave.

UPI Photo

Children waiting for food outside a government station in East Pakistan (now Bangladesh), November 22, 1970.

There is not one continent in the world that does not have the resources to be able to adequately feed, clothe, and house every one of its people. Yet, most of the leaders, victims of the demagogue's disease, lack the wisdom or the desire to find the solution.

Illegally built shanties in the Tondo District of Manila, the Philippines. October 22, 1972.

First Lady of the Philippines and governor of metropolitan Manila, Mrs. Imelda Marcos, throws a pair of dice at a new floating gambling casino as actress Gina Lollobrigida and President Ferdinand Marcos (to Gina's left) look on. Manila Bay, January 1, 1976.

It is not easy to overthrow a dictator, particularly when he has the military on his side.

UPI Photo

Iranian students in the United States wearing masks during their demonstrations for fear that the Iranian secret police will identify them and penalize their families. New York City, July 7, 1977.

The Shah of Iran (center with glasses) surrounded by cheering supporters in Tehran on December 4, 1978. What is not apparent in the picture is that the demonstration was held at the Iranian Air Force Training Center in Tehran, where the officers and their wives were expected to give an enthusiastic welcome to the Shah. In the U.S., Presidents Johnson and Nixon would arrange similarly "enthusiastic" receptions for themselves on military bases when they sensed that they were losing favor with the American people. Six weeks after this picture was taken, the Shah was forced to flee his country.

Who are the people who take to the streets with placards and angry shouts to protest against what they consider to be incompetent, unfeeling, and unwise politicians? Are they all left-wing radical students? No. They are workers . . .

UPI Photo

Thousands of workers gather in the Piazza del Duomo in Milan, Italy, during a general strike called to protest rising unemployment and widespread economic chaos. March 25, 1976.

... political exiles ...

Exiles from the Dominican Republic stage a demonstration in New York City on July 28, 1960, voicing their hatred of Dominican dictator Rafael Trujillo. A year later, Trujillo was assassinated.

... mothers and housewives ...

Thousands of women take to the streets of Santiago, Chile, to protest chronic food shortages. September 11, 1973.

... farmers ...

A "tractorcade" heads for downtown Wichita, Kansas, to demonstrate farmers' dissatisfaction with the agricultural policies of President Carter. October 21, 1978.

... doctors ...

Armed police in Buenos Aires, Argentina, lead arrested demonstrators away from the Plaza de Mayo (in front of the Presidential Palace), following a march by doctors protesting against high prices and low salaries. July 23, 1975.

... and outraged citizens of every kind.

More than 10,000 persons in Managua, Nicaragua, attend the burial of Pedro Joaquin Chamorro, publisher of *La Prensa,* an anti-government newspaper, who was assassinated two days earlier. The demonstration is an implicit protest against the repressive government of President Anastasio Somoza. January 12, 1978.

Unfortunately, general strikes and many other forms of social protest grind the whole economy to a halt, so that the people hurt themselves in the attempt to bring down or alter their political leadership. How much more productive it would be if the whole institution of career politics could be abolished!

UPI Photo

The main hall at Retiro, Buenos Aires' largest railroad station, is empty of trains and commuters as a crippling nationwide strike grips Argentina, leaving the economy in shambles. 9:36 A.M., July 7, 1975.

Whenever universities are ordered closed, it is a certain sign that the political leaders are more concerned with keeping themselves in power than with developing a nation of people who will be able to think and work in the modern world.

Police stand guard over hundreds of student protesters at Thammasat University in Bangkok, Thailand, October 6, 1976.

Whenever political leaders don't know what card to play next, they always remember that clubs are trumps.

Philippine riot police clubbing students who had demonstrated against cutbacks in funds to education. Manila, January 30, 1970.

Philippine students seeking refuge in one of their vehicles as the anti-Marcos demonstration continues. Manila, February 10, 1970.

Imitating the violence used by politicians, desperate citizens sometimes resort to assassination.

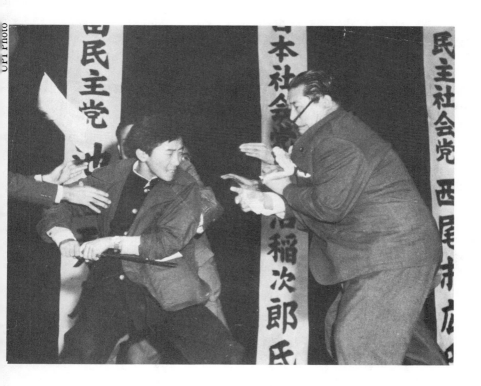

Japanese Socialist leader Inejiro Asanuma vainly tries to protect himself as his assassin withdraws his dagger to lunge again. Tokyo, October 12, 1960.

The demagogue's disease is in an advanced stage when a political leader padlocks his Congress and arrests his rivals and critics.

UPI Photo

Northern Luzon Congressman Roque Ablan (left) and Governor David Puzon (right, inside the gate), of Cagayan, are among those placed behind bars by President Marcos of the Philippines. Here, they are bidding goodbye to friends at Camp Aguinaldo, Manila, October 1, 1972.

The jailing of political leaders has become a common occurrence throughout the world. In most cases, the jailing or official execution of past presidents and prime ministers comes about by virtue of the oppressive tactics which those leaders had used to keep themselves in power.

UPI Photo

Former Indian Prime Minister Indira Gandhi being released from the Tihar jail in New Delhi on December 26, 1978. Undoubtedly, Mrs. Gandhi, like most other career politicians in the world, will continue to yearn for the power and glory of high office and will keep seeking to be reelected.

The ballot box, which was once the hope of depressed peoples everywhere, is fast becoming a farce because the choices are generally limited to mediocre career politicians. In the United States, elections are regarded as meaningless by so many people that the level of voter turnout has fallen below that in every other democracy except Botswana.

Native voters carrying ballot boxes for the February 1972 election in the eastern highlands of Papua New Guinea.

Whatever their color, politicians are the burden of us all.

UPI Photo

Uganda's President-for-life Idi Amin Dada, a former cook and heavy-weight boxer, being carried on a makeshift throne by four Englishmen to an official reception in Kampala, Uganda, July 18, 1975.

UPI Photo

Englishman Roland James Moxon serving as a chief in the village of On-
yaase, Ghana. July 15, 1969.

In the past, the world could tolerate the demagogue's disease
—if not happily, at least with survival. Today, the political
leaders of the world have at their disposal weapons of such
destructive power that for the first time in the course of civili-
zation a war could end life on Earth.

UPI Photo

Explosion of the atomic bomb on Bikini Atoll, July 25, 1946.

The Author

As a Regent of the University of California, Edward A. Morris (left) served as the Vice-Chairman of the committee that oversees the research laboratories in which the nuclear weapons of the United States are developed. In that capacity, he became uniquely familiar with the precariousness of human survival in the nuclear age. While the "father" of the H-bomb, Dr. Edward Teller (facing left), converses in the background, the author inspects a kilogram of pure plutonium. It was at just about this time that he became determined to write this book. Los Alamos, New Mexico, June 10, 1976. (Photo courtesy of the Los Alamos Scientific Laboratory.)

Dialogue

Numerous questions have been put to me over the years in the course of my lectures, conversations, and correspondence with a wide variety of people in many nations and from various levels of society. So many questions have been asked, in fact, that I have thought it best to present my answers in the form of a dialogue. I have arranged the order of the questions and edited them grammatically, but in other respects they are essentially in their original form. My answers, on the other hand, are extended versions of my original impromptu responses, though I have retained the original conversational style and tone.

I would like to note at the outset that I have encountered objections of every kind from every side. I have spoken with governors, senators, and congressmen, with eminent scientists and educators, with military and business leaders, with artists, with presidents and ministers of foreign countries, with political prisoners—in short, with powerful extraordinary people and with powerless ordinary people in virtually every walk of life—and everywhere my ideas have been greeted with emotional support but intellectual misgivings. I have made no attempt to conceal the adversary nature of many of these questions, however, nor have I suppressed any that might appear to weaken my argument. It is my hope that at the very least I can persuade the reader to reexamine the political institutions of his own country (or state) and consider how the application of my proposals could make improvements upon them.

Finally, let me say that I view the dialogue as an ongoing one. Should readers wish to pose questions of their own or to make comments, I would be more than happy to consider including the most relevant and incisive ones in a later edition of this book. Letters should be addressed to me at Suite 3400, 555 California Street, San Francisco, California 94104.

* * *

Question: *Mr. Morris, how did you first conceive of the demagogue's disease and its cure?*

Answer: The concept did not occur to me all at once; it came in parts after a great deal of thought. Even now, I still modify the details from time to time, though the overall solution to the problem has been clear to me for quite a while.

I suppose my earliest formal ideas on the subject sprang out of my reflections on the causes of war. I spent a great deal of time, some years ago, studying literally hundreds of proposals that have been put forth over the centuries for the elimination of war from the affairs of mankind. Many of these plans were quite excellent, and I was forced to conclude that it was not the plans that were defective but the leaders who are called upon to follow them. Their desire for power and glory, for which I later coined the term "demagogue's disease," was clearly at the bottom of the problem. So, too, was the element of fear. This I realized as I stood one day on a balcony beside a prominent government official. While both of us were looking at a crowd of people below, one of the leader's bodyguards whispered that it would be prudent for him to stand back from the edge, so that no one in the crowd could get a good shot at him. As he stepped back, I remained at the railing alone and thought about all the high-ranking officials in this and other countries who must constantly fear for themselves and their families. In many lands, that fear is not only of the masses but of the leader's own inner circle—perhaps a coup by his generals. Such fear, I thought, is bound to warp one's thinking—and consequently one's decision-making powers. How, I wondered, could we eliminate or reduce this fear among our public servants? That question tied in with an earlier idea I had that short-term nonprofessional office-holders would be a great deal more varied in experience, knowledge, and skill than the long-term professional politicians we have today. The rest of the theoretical plant, so to speak, grew from these seeds.

Q: *Won't your proposal to limit political tenure take the professionalism—in the best sense of that word—out of politics and turn all politicians into amateurs?*

A: Do you think that if the president of a large corporation— a man who deals with power relationships every day—were to enter politics, we could rightly consider him a political amateur? I doubt it, and I think the same thing could be said for labor leaders, minority spokesmen, women's rights advocates, educators, and others. It is not necessary for one to have been in government to understand political infighting, on the one hand, or to be a professional administrator or legislator, on the other. In fact, what I want to see is a broader professional input into politics, rather than relying so heavily, as now, upon politically ambitious lawyers. What we need in our leaders is the quality of wisdom, and we are more likely to find it among the successful people in nonpolitical careers than among those who work their way up through petty party politics to high political office. Most so-called professional politicians are poorly qualified to solve the problems of this or any other country, and are highly qualified principally at fence-straddling and putting the best possible face on everything they do, in the hope of getting themselves reelected.

> *The world is growing weary of that most costly of all luxuries, heredity kings.*
>
> —George Bancroft, 1848

Q: *How can you hope to persuade current officeholders to back such an idea when to do so would be political and perhaps economic suicide?*

A: That's really no problem. Just as President Truman was exempted from the provisions of the Twenty-second Amendment to the Constitution, which restricted a President to two terms, so all present officeholders would be exempted from the provisions of a constitutional amendment limiting political officeholding to a specific length of time. In other words, the amendment would contain what is called a grandfather's clause. Anyone in political office prior to the adoption of the amendment would be allowed to remain in politics indefinitely.

Q: *Won't that create bitter infighting and perhaps outright chaos during the transition period? With new politicians limited to a specific number of years in office, won't the power naturally stay with the old-timers? The newcomers might then have to spend half their time or more either doing battle with or currying favor from the established forces, and the whole purpose of your proposal would be undermined.*

A: By the time this country—or any other country—enacts a constitutional amendment designed to combat the demagogue's disease, the electorate will have become pretty well convinced that something drastic needs to be done about the problem. Such an enlightened electorate will start weeding out the old-timers protected by the grandfather's clause. They will weed them out in the same way that obviously unwanted politicians have always been weeded out in a democracy—at the ballot box.

Q: *The present Congress is loaded with freshman congressmen. Isn't that a sign that the ballot box is working pretty well right now, without help from your proposal?*

A: That's a transitory phenomenon. The question is, how long is it going to last? After two years, most of those freshman congressmen will get reelected. Two years after that, they'll get reelected again. And twenty years from now, they'll still be in office, only not so fresh anymore, and the system won't have changed a bit. In fact, even the original freshness is mostly illusion, for many of those new congressmen have been playing politics at the state level for years. Why must we go on like that? If it's good to have amateur politicians in there now, let's enable "amateurs" to be in there all the time.

Q: *How will the amateur politician be able to resist the arguments and demands of the military lobby?*

A: First of all, please take into consideration that the original meaning of the word *amateur* was not someone who was ignorant of what he was doing, but rather someone who did what he did out of love—from the Latin *amator,* "lover." My notion of the kind of political officeholder who will emerge under the new system is someone who will put his love for his country above all other consid-

> *If the king says at noonday, "It is night," the wise man says, "Behold the stars!"*
>
> —Persian proverb

erations. He will not be interested in having a military installation named after him or desire to puff up his ego by inspecting brass bands. His concern will be simply to see to it that his country is as strong as it needs to be to protect its vital interests. There is no reason why he will have to rely solely on the word of the military lobbyists, even on military issues of great technological complexity. There will always be plenty of expert spokesmen from all sides, and the elected official's job will be to arrive at a wise judgment after listening to *all* sides.

Q: *What do you think will happen if some countries adopt your solution and others do not? Will we then have novices on one side negotiating with seasoned professionals on the other?*

A: That is very unlikely. Our State Department and the foreign ministries of other countries around the world will continue to be staffed by professionals. My solution applies only to *elected* officials.

Q: *In American television there is mediocrity in programming because that's apparently what most of the people want. Doesn't the mediocrity of our politicians flow from the same source— namely, the appeal to the lowest common denominator?*

A: But that's precisely what my proposal is designed to correct. I want to see the *best* people in politics, and I want them to appeal to our highest ideals rather than our lowest instincts. Today, mediocre politicians, following the Peter Principle, rise to their level of incompetence. Tomorrow, after tenure has been limited, excellent leaders will contribute a few years of their lives to politics and then return to their original vocations.

The founding fathers never envisioned that people would go into politics and make a career out of it for twenty or thirty years or more. This is one of the ways that modern science has backfired on us and threatened our form of democracy. By making politicians —as well as everyone else—live longer, medical science has helped to perpetuate mediocrity and incompetence in high places.

Q: *But isn't there an antidemocratic tendency in your philosophy? You don't seem to trust the judgment of the people.*

A: Do you really believe that the people are putting up the candidates today? Of course they aren't. Most of the time, they find themselves voting, not for their choice, but for the lesser of two evils—provided they bother to vote at all.* The success of Jimmy Carter in the 1976 presidential campaign was a clear signal from the people that they were fed up with the old ways. It's true that their honeymoon with Carter didn't last very long, but the point here is not specific personalities; rather it is that the people were struggling to express a long-felt discontent, and Carter was merely

---

*A study by the *Los Angeles Times* shows that the national elections of November 7, 1978 "produced one of the lowest voter turnouts in history, about 37 percent, which was even lower than the 38.5 percent recorded in 1974 in the midst of Watergate-inspired disillusionment" (*San Francisco Chronicle,* November 10, 1978). According to Curtis B. Gans, Director of the Committee for the Study of the American Electorate, "the level of voter turnout in the U.S. has fallen below every other democracy except Botswana" (*Newsweek,* October 30, 1978, p. 33).

> *Idealism is the noble toga that political*
> *gentlemen drape over their will to power.*
>
> —Aldous Huxley, 1963

shrewd enough to ride that sentiment to victory. Unless we take note of that underlying discontent, however, and take measures to correct the system itself, rather than merely changing the names of the people at the top, things will only get worse.

But to speak directly to what you call my "antidemocratic tendency," I would say that I *do* trust the judgment of the people, but more in the long run than in the short run. In the short run, the people can be fooled by charlatans. As Lincoln said, "You can fool some of the people all of the time, and all of the people some of the time." My idea is to make it more difficult to fool *any* of the people *any* of the time.

Q: *What about the occasional career politician who is really good? Why should we set up a system that has no room for him?*

A: True, one out of a hundred may be very good, and we're going to lose him under this system. It's more important, however, to spare ourselves the ninety-nine incompetents. Besides, the truly good politician needn't leave public service entirely. He can become a political consultant, or elected officials might recognize his worth and appoint him to some advisory position. We should be more concerned with the people in this society who are being deprived because of the demagogues than about the few disappointed demagogues who won't be able to play the political game for the rest of their lives.

Q: *What is to prevent corrupt politicians from simply speeding up their corruption in the shorter time allowed to them?*

A: In the first place, the kind of people attracted to political office will be entirely different. Rather than being career politicians trained early in the arts of compromise and corruption, they will be successful individuals from nonpolitical fields to which they will ultimately return. Thus the chance that they will become corrupt *before* running for high political office will be reduced to a minimum. Furthermore, it's unlikely that they will become corrupt *while* in office, because they will know that on that certain day when they must step down forever, their activities will be carefully scrutinized by their successors. They'll always be aware that, should any corruption be found, they'll end up spending a good part of their post-political years in jail.

Q: *Aren't there other people aside from politicians who can gain immense power and pose a threat to nations or the world? I am thinking particularly of popes and United States Supreme Court justices. Don't you think they can contract the demagogue's disease, and if so, do you want to limit their terms of office, too?*

A: It seems to me that for someone to succumb to the demagogue's disease in a socially dangerous way, he must be surrounded *both* by power *and* by glory. For example, the Lord Mayor of London may get to ride in magnificent processions, decked out with robes in a golden carriage, but he has very little political power. Thus, even if he were allowed to stay in office for his entire lifetime, instead of the one year he is limited to now, it would do society very little harm.

Supreme Court justices, on the other hand, certainly do have real power, but in their case the *glory* of the office is muted.

> *Power gradually extirpates from the mind
> every humane and gentle virtue.*
>
> —Edmund Burke, 1756

They have an obligation to conduct themselves with dignity, avoid notoriety, and generally remain out of the public eye in their private lives. Also, they have very little time to be out seeking more *power*, since today's Supreme Court justices are extremely overworked and their rulings are under daily scrutiny by some of the finest legal minds in the country. Furthermore, by the time someone is appointed to this lofty bench, he is usually advanced in years, and therefore probably beyond the petty ambitiousness of a younger man. Aside from all these theoretical reasons, however, I simply can't think of a single case in history where a Supreme Court justice went around grandstanding before the public in order to puff up his own power and stature. William Howard Taft went from the presidency to the Supreme Court, but no one, so far as I know, has ever attempted to go in the other direction.

As for popes, they also generally come to office at an advanced age; they are frequently a political compromise between the various factions of the Catholic Church, which means that more often than not, at least in recent times, they tend to be relatively apolitical; and, most important of all, it is incumbent upon them, as Christ's official representatives on Earth, to act with humility.

Thus, though I'm not certain that I *wouldn't* rather see popes and Supreme Court justices restricted to limited terms, the fact that they're not so limited doesn't particularly trouble me.

Q: *What about the leaders of the great labor unions? If a John L. Lewis or a Jimmy Hoffa or a George Meany gets the demagogue's disease—as you'll probably agree all of them did—doesn't that adversely affect a great segment of society?*

A: It's true that the men you named all exerted enormous power in society, and Meany in his eighties still does. However, as we've seen with Hoffa, there are certain checks on their power. If they go too far in one direction, they get in trouble with the law; if they go too far in another direction, they get in trouble with other union leaders; and if they go too far in a third direction, they get in trouble with the underworld. But beyond this, let me say that it is my ultimate hope that limited tenures of office *will* one day be extended to such organizations as labor unions. Once the nation has recognized the demagogue's disease in the political sphere and done something about it, then the time will come when the same principles will be applied to other levels of society.

Q: *But why are you limiting your attack to politicians when, in fact, some labor union leaders are more powerful than many congressmen or even senators?*

A: Frankly, it's really a matter of timing. If I were to come out and attack labor union leaders, I suppose the next thing I would have to do would be to attack corporation presidents, the heads of charitable organizations, school principals, university presidents, and so on. I'm afraid we would soon reach a point where so many people would be fearful of the change I'm advocating that no one would want to take even the first step in overhauling society— namely, placing limits on political careers. It is not my purpose to alienate everyone in sight. I simply want to point out that the problem is particularly acute in the political sphere, and that is

> *The lust for power, for dominating others,*
> *inflames the heart more than any other*
> *passion.*
>
> —Tacitus, ca. 115 A.D.

where I wish to focus my energies at the present time.

Q: *Could you be more precise than you have been up to now about the number of years you would like to see political officeholders limited to?*

A: My own preference is to limit people to between six and eight years in elective office, but I try to avoid referring to some absolute number of years because I believe there's room for negotiation on that, and also because the issue is complicated by proposals for altering the present length of terms of office. For example, there has long been a debate about whether or not to extend the term of members of the House of Representatives, and if so, whether three or four years would be preferable. I personally would find either extension a vast improvement over the present two-year term that requires congressmen to run for reelection every other year. As for senators, I would like to see them limited to one term, but whether it should be for the current six years or be reduced to, say, four or five years, is subject to what happens in the House.

In general, I would like to see politicians at the federal level limited to two terms in Congress: either to two terms in the House or to one term in the House and one in the Senate. Under the present system, that would mean serving for a total of either four or eight years. But if we increased a congressman's term to three years and reduced a senator's to five, the choice would be between six and eight years. All these details can be worked out if we always keep in mind the ultimate objective: namely, the elimination of career politics.

Q: *What about politicians at the state, county, and city levels of government? Would you also like to see them limited to six or eight years in elective office?*

A: Yes, I would, at least insofar as full-time positions are concerned. However, this matter is not so pressing, since there is much less power and glory at those lower levels of government, and therefore the demagogue's disease is not quite so rampant or destructive.

Q: *You say that the demagogue's disease is less rampant and less destructive below the federal level of government. But aren't the mayors of major cities and the governors of major states just as susceptible to the disease as any congressman, if not more so?*

A: You're quite right. I was thinking of the thousands of politicians at the state, county, and city levels who are mostly unheard-of outside their own constituencies, rather than the handful of celebrities who govern a few major cities and states. The latter can indeed catch just as big a case of the demagogue's disease as any congressman, if not bigger. Sometimes they even announce the presence of their disease in bold letters on what I call the political quarantine sign—for example, "Welcome to Chicago from Mayor Richard J. Daley," when the sign could just as easily have said: "Welcome to the City from the People of Chicago."

     A few politicians, to be sure, dislike "quarantine signs" which proclaim their own egotism, and they take steps to have the

> *The only prize much cared for by the powerful is power. The prize of the general is not a bigger tent, but command.*
>
> —Oliver Wendell Holmes, Jr.

signs removed. To come back to your question, however, and to what may have been the motivation behind your asking it: Yes, the mayors of major cities and the governors of major states are special cases, since they tend to be constantly in the news and since they wield substantial power. Nevertheless, it would not be practical to apply special regulations to them so that, say, the mayor of New York City would be allowed less time in office than the mayor of, say, Pocatello, Idaho, even though we may all agree that the mayor of the larger city is more likely to contract the disease.

Q: *If someone were to move from the city, county, or state to the federal level of government, would you count their lower-level time against them, or would you only limit them to a specific number of years at each level?*

A: I would count their total time in elective office against them, irrespective of level. Thus, if someone were, say, the mayor of a city for four years, those years would count against him when he later becomes, say, the governor of his state. However, I am not totally opposed to the idea that from two to four years of officeholding below the federal level might be discounted in the case of candidates for federal office.

Q: *Why not simply limit politicians to a specific number of years at any one level of government? Isn't that a good way for them to gain a variety of government experience and for the best of them to rise from lower to higher levels?*

A: Again, the major underlying principle behind my proposal is that there should be no professional politicians in elective office. It is because of the professionalization of politics that politicians are more concerned with their public relations than with their public service. Furthermore, if we continue to have officeholders working their way up the political ladder, we'll only be perpetuating a system in which the majority of the people at the top have risen to their own levels of incompetence.

   If you look at their histories, you'll find that most of today's senators were previously congressmen, most congressmen were previously state legislators, most state legislators were previously county officials, and so on down the line. Scratch deep enough into their past and you'll usually find a young mediocre lawyer with few clients and a lot of time on his hands. When he becomes, say, a councilman in a small town, he's content to spend many nights down at the city hall debating such minor issues as where to install parking meters. In other words, he's not what you could call a big thinker. On the contrary, he's a small-time operator, and an old expression applies to his kind: "If you don't give people important things to do, they'll start regarding as important the things you *do* give them to do." Now, petty politicians certainly regard the things they do as important, but I don't believe that's the proper background for someone who's later going to help decide the fate of this nation and perhaps the world.

Q: *But what about the other way around, with high officials later assuming lower positions? Beginning with President John*

> *Unlimited power is apt to corrupt the minds of those who possess it.*
>
> —William Pitt, 1770

Quincy Adams going into the House of Representatives, this nation has had such a tradition of public service.

A: I think that's very much the exception. Very few people in the world seek to move down in power, and this nation can well afford to lose the elective services of those who do. But don't forget, my proposal applies only to *elected* officials, and not to cabinet members, political advisers, civil servants, or other persons who serve at the pleasure of their superiors rather than at the pleasure of the population at large. For elected officials there would still be the option of going into *non*elective government service. For example, former President Hoover was appointed by President Truman to chair the Famine Emergency Commission, which helped the starving people of Europe and Asia after World War II. Later, President Eisenhower appointed Hoover chairman of the Committee on Reorganization of United States Executive Departments. That kind of thing is fine because the appointee is freed from electioneering and can truly devote his time to public service worthy of the name.

Q: *You are yourself an attorney, and yet you seem to be very hostile to attorneys who go into politics. Why is that?*

A: *Hostility* is the wrong word to use to describe my attitude, because it suggests that I have something personal against these people, which is certainly not the case. I am opposed to their incompetence and their mediocrity when they're in politics, because I believe that the nation needs and deserves better. But it is not the lawyers as such that I am opposed to, only lawyers who are typically drawn to politics because their private practices are going nowhere. Yet, even if these people were the best lawyers in the world, I would still like to see more non-lawyers in government service. Why should three-quarters of the nation's politicians be attorneys, and hardly one a scientist or worker or housewife?

Some years ago, in connection with an article I was writing about lawyers in politics ("Lawyers and Scientists," *Journal of the State Bar of California,* 38 [July 1963],458), I did some research into the question of why there were so few scientists in Congress. At that time, there was only one person in either house of Congress who by any stretch of the imagination could have been considered a scientist, and that was Hubert Humphrey, who had once been a pharmacist. Today, with former astronaut John Glenn sitting in the Senate, the situation is about the same as it was then—and workers and housewives aren't doing any better. What we need in government is diversity and excellence, not narrowness and mediocrity.

Q: *You've quoted the late Congressman Leo Ryan as saying that most congressmen spend about ten months out of every two-year term campaigning for reelection. What's so bad about having the politicians devoting half of their time checking with their constituents and mending their political fences? Isn't that the way democracy is supposed to work?*

A: There's nothing wrong with politicians checking with their constituencies, as you call it, except that, more often than not, that's a euphemism for holding back-room conferences with political bosses, pressure groups, big campaign contributors, and their own biased campaign workers. And when they're not doing that, they're

> *Power tends to corrupt; absolute power corrupts absolutely.*
>
> —Lord Acton, 1887

out making speeches designed to make themselves look good and their political opponents look bad. Even at supposedly intimate political gatherings, the politician typically struts in amid applause, "works the room" by shaking hands with a few people, gives a twenty-minute speech, and departs again amid applause. This kind of charade cannot be called a dialogue with the voters. I fail to see how such activities either reflect the will of the people, on the one hand, or shed any light on the pressing social problems of our day, on the other. If politicians could be freed to quietly concentrate on those problems without a lot of grandstanding and hoopla, more of the problems would get solved.

Q: *But under your proposal, members of Congress would still have to campaign twice. How would they be free of electioneering?*

A: As President Eisenhower said, people running for political office under the new system would tend to think of politics as an interlude in their lives rather than as a way of making a living. Thus, the prospect of losing an election would not be so terrifying as it is to most career politicians today. A person would win or lose on the basis of his principles, and not on his ability to manipulate the public's vulnerabilities.

Let's remember that in the early days of this country, there was no such thing as consensus politics. A man ran for office on a platform that he believed in, and he won or lost accordingly. Today, at a time when political campaigns are run by advertising agencies that use the same techniques for promoting candidates that they use for selling products, a politician is almost necessarily one thing in public and another thing in private. The best example of that in recent times was Richard Nixon, but he was only one of many public relations products to be merchandised to the American people in this age of television.

I'm not saying that a politician shouldn't look at the polls and see what the people want. Of course he should. He's a representative of the people and he must take their desires into account. But he's also more than a mere nose counter. If he weren't, he could be replaced by a computer. He *can't* be replaced by a computer precisely because the people have elected him to spend his time becoming familiar with the urgent problems of the day and exercising his best *judgment*—on their behalf—to solve them. We all know that the world's problems today are nothing short of monumental, and they're not going to be solved by people who have to spend half of their time figuring out how to make themselves popular.

Q: *It can be argued that congressmen are no longer policymakers but are now mostly ombudsmen for their constituents vis-à-vis the bureaucracy. How would you respond to that argument?*

A: I'm afraid the argument is more or less true. For the most part, congressmen have yielded up their policymaking role to the executive and judicial branches; but at the same time, unfortunately, they're not very good ombudsmen either. First, in their desire to take over the entire social system and regulate everything in sight, the politicians created a monstrous bureaucracy with all sorts of agencies that never should have come into existence in the first place. Then, with frustrated constituents screaming to them for help against the bureaucratic nightmare, the congressmen try to undo some of the political tangle on a one-by-one basis for the few

> *Power, like a desolating pestilence, pollutes whate'er it touches.*
>
> —Percy Bysshe Shelley, 1813

people who can reach their ear. In the meantime, the country and the world sink further and further into chaos.

Q: *Your focus up to now has been mostly on members of Congress. Is it your belief that the presidency has been immunized from the demagogue's disease by the Twenty-second Amendment's imposition of the two-term limitation?*

A: No, not under the present system, as we have so unfortunately seen in recent administrations. Of course, it's a good thing that Presidents have been limited to two terms; but as things are now, they can still be—and usually are—career politicians, ascending to the presidency after years in politics at other levels. I suggest that a presidential candidate be allowed to serve a maximum of eight years in prior political office. On top of that, I would advocate that the presidency itself be limited to *one* term. My own preference would be to have one four-year term, but one six-year term might also be acceptable.

In fact, a lot of people over the years have favored the idea of one six-year presidential term. Since the Constitution was ratified, hundreds of amendments have been introduced in Congress proposing a change in presidential tenure, and more than 130 of these proposed amendments have recommended a single term of six years.* In more recent times, Richard Nixon argued, when he

---

*See list in Appendix D.

was Vice-President, that the presidency should be limited to one six-year term because, he said, Presidents enjoy the position so much and want to keep the job so badly that they often neglect running the government during the first four years while they plan strategies to win the next election. Later, when Nixon was President, he certainly proved his thesis. Even more recently, John Connally, the former governor of Texas, urged a constitutional amendment to limit Presidents to a single six-year term, and President Carter and Attorney General Griffin B. Bell are also speaking out in favor of the idea.

In any case, it was certainly not my intention to give the impression that the presidency is immune to the demagogue's disease because of the Twenty-second Amendment. In fact, if a constitutional convention is called in the near future, I shall strongly urge that additional tenure limitations be placed on the presidency as well as on all other elective offices.

Q: *It is the Executive branch of government, not the Congress, that runs the day-to-day affairs of this country. Furthermore, many of the members of the Cabinet, the National Security Council, the Council of Economic Advisers, and other presidential appointees seem to be exactly the kind of political "amateurs" that you've been calling for in the Congress. Therefore, what's so wrong with the present system the way it is?*

A: It's true that Cabinet members and other presidential appointees are often highly qualified leaders from the business world, the universities, the labor unions, and other nongovernmental and nonpolitical arenas, and many of them are precisely the type of political "amateur" that I've been recommending for government service. However, these people do not have the kind of autonomy that an elected official has. They are answerable to the President,

> *Today the nations of the world may be*
> *divided into two classes—the nations in*
> *which the government fears the people, and*
> *the nations in which the people fear the*
> *government.*
>
> —Amos R. E. Pinchot, 1935

on the one hand, and to Congress, on the other. They must of necessity be team players, which means, in effect, that they must always make the President look good, never embarrass him, and keep one eye continually on his reelection. Even if this were not so, and they were totally free to do whatever they thought was in the best interests of the country regardless of the effect upon the President's popularity, they would still have to face a Congress that *is*, under the present system, excessively concerned with *its* reelection. Thus, the best policies in the world can't do much good if they're not backed up by funds and enabling legislation provided by the Congress.

We saw this recently in respect to the energy question. Energy Secretary James Schlesinger mapped out a comprehensive energy policy that would have required the nation to face up to some very unpleasant realities. By the time the program got past the hurdles put up by all the politicians around the country, there wasn't much left of the original plan. So it's not enough to eliminate the demagogue's disease in only one part of the body politic, any more than it would be enough to remove cancer from only one part of the physical body. The whole political structure is organically interconnected, and if the demagogue's disease is to be thoroughly eradicated, the cure will have to be taken throughout the system.

Q: *You have said that one presidential term, whether of four or six years, would allow the President to do what is in the very best interests of the country, since he would not have to worry about getting reelected. Why wouldn't that same argument apply to the second four-year term as we have it now?*

A: To some extent it does. For example, it's been reported that President Kennedy planned to phase out the Vietnam War after his hoped-for reelection in 1964. In other words, he considered pulling out the right thing to do, but his fear of not getting reelected prevented him from doing it in his first term. The consequences of that fear proved to be horrendous for the nation, and we might well have been spared the agony of that nightmare had there been no such thing as a second presidential term. Furthermore, Watergate would probably never have occurred if President Nixon and his aides had not been obsessed with *his* reelection.
      But to answer your question in a more general way, I should add that the political environment surrounding a one-term President would be somewhat different from and superior to that of a President serving his second and last term. From the very start, a one-term President would not have to make campaign and image strategists an intimate part of his team, as Presidents do today. Moreover, all across the board, a one-term President would not have to make political appointments based on "cronyism" and in payment of past and future campaign debts, but could choose people strictly on merit. All this is in addition to the general fact that devoted "amateurs" would be taking the place of self-promoting professionals in government; so, as with congressmen and senators, the *quality* of Presidents (and presidential candidates) would be higher than it is today.

Q: *What about a President who pursued unpopular policies throughout his one term? Without the possibility of voting him out, what check would the people have on his excesses?*

> *Whenever a man has cast a longing eye on offices, a rottenness begins in his conduct.*
>
> —Thomas Jefferson, 1820

A: Let's not forget, first of all, that Congress would still have the power of impeachment to check any gross offenses, though not, of course, simply to punish unpopularity. Furthermore, an unpopular President would have great trouble getting any of his programs through Congress, so he'd have to make some concessions if he wanted to get anything accomplished. On top of that, every President is concerned about how he will be judged by future generations, and it's likely that he would want to go down in history as a good President. Finally, as I have already indicated, a President is part of a team, and if he wants to have some influence over who succeeds him and over the shape of his successor's policies, he will have to pass on a more or less popular legacy. Taking all these factors into account, I'm not at all worried that a one-term President will deliberately pursue policies with no regard for the will of the people, the Congress, or the courts. To the contrary, thanks to the higher caliber of persons entering politics under the new system, Presidents will have more concern than ever for the welfare of the nation and its institutions.

Q: *What is your attitude toward Franklin Delano Roosevelt, the only President of the United States ever to serve more than two terms?*

A: Although there is a lot to admire in Roosevelt's presidency, there is no doubt in my mind that he had the demagogue's disease, particularly after his landslide victory in 1936. But even if he hadn't contracted the demagogue's disease, he wasn't in the best of *physical* health during his third and fourth terms, just at the time when he was making decisions and entering into international agreements that shaped the postwar world for years, if not decades, to come. Perhaps if we had had someone more vigorous in office at that time, we might have a better world today.

In any case, after the Roosevelt experience, the people decided in retrospect that an open-ended presidency was unhealthy for the nation, and so the Congress and the states enacted the Twenty-second Amendment to the Constitution, limiting our Presidents to two terms. I believe that was a needed change in our Constitution, and now we have need for another to apply similar limits to politicians in general.

Q: *What would happen to party politics under the new system? Would there continue to be parties?*

A: Certainly. There were parties in the first hundred years of this nation, even though the politicians were only spending an average of four years in office. There's no reason why party politics must necessarily produce career politicians. In fact, in the absence of career politicians, parties may even become stronger than they are now. In their more active search for the best leaders, since they will no longer have a stable of old hacks to draw from, they will bring together people who are aligned more by political philosophy than by political self-interest, and this will tend to give the parties a greater cohesion.

Q: *Do you want the two-party system to remain in the United States?*

> *Contact with the affairs of state is one of the most corrupting of the influences to which men are exposed.*
>
> —James Fenimore Cooper, 1838

A: I have mixed feelings about that point, but I suppose that's alright, since my advocacy position doesn't require me to take sides on that issue any more than someone advocating the cure of cancer must necessarily take the side of private or socialized medicine. On the one hand, I like the adversary nature of American politics, with two strong parties competing for the hearts and minds of the American people. On the other hand, a great deal of ideological diversity gets lost in these political melting pots. Having at least three strong competitors seems to work well in private industry (for example, in automobile manufacture and network television), so perhaps three strong political parties wouldn't be a bad idea. We couldn't have many more than three, however, or we'd have difficulty achieving a workable government majority.

Q: *Would it be fair to say that what you're trying to do is to get philosopher-kings out of Plato's imaginary republic and into our real one?*

A: Leaving Plato's antidemocratic bias aside, and assuming that *king* is understood metaphorically, I'd say yes. What we need is to devise a way to get philosopher-kings into office, and to see to it that once they're in they remain philosophers without becoming tyrants or demagogues. The most important virtue for a politician, in my opinion, is wisdom. He needn't be a specialist on constitutional law, or economics, or military affairs, or whatever. There will be plenty of experts and staff members who will be able to bring him the relevant information on those matters. Instead, he should be the political equivalent of the old general practitioner in medicine. He should be aware of the big picture and weigh matters with his heart as well as his head. He should put his country's interests first and his own last. And he should remember at all times that he is the people's servant and never their master. If that adds up to what Plato called a philosopher-king, then that is what I want.

Q: *You have indicated that high officials are often ill-informed. What do you think makes that so?*

A: Part of the reason, I believe, is that a leader's views narrow the longer he stays in public office. This comes about in several ways. First, advisers to a leader, no matter how brilliant they may be, are chosen because they share a certain viewpoint; and people with one viewpoint tend to reinforce their common biases. Also, high officials are generally too busy to consult all segments of society and are isolated by layers of bureaucracy. Add to this the fear of assassination and the tendency to gradually withdraw within one's inner circle of close supporters, and it will not be too long before a leader is seriously out of touch with his people.

I believe that, all too often, national leaders do not see the true picture of what is happening in their country. Truth is like a mosaic: it is made up of an infinite number of perspectives; it can never be found in just one place—not in legislative halls, scientific laboratories, classrooms, exclusive clubs, the marketplace, the farms, the factories, or the ghettoes. But important parts of it can be found in *all* of these places, and to the extent that a searcher tries to look everywhere, to that extent will his picture of truth be more complete.

> *You can't adopt politics as a profession and remain honest.*
>
> —L. M. Howe, 1933

So when I am asked why I believe that a politician representing a poor constituency should spend time getting to really know the rich, or why a politician representing a rich constituency should make a real effort to learn from the poor, my answer is that the more groups of people a leader truly understands, the closer he will come to that most elusive of political virtues—wisdom.

Q: *You have mentioned wisdom a number of times. Why do you assume that our leaders are going to be wise simply because their tenure is limited?*

A: I'm not suggesting that an unwise politician will suddenly become wise when we limit his tenure. What I am saying is that when there are no more career politicians, the people who go into politics will be successful leaders from other fields. Thus, by limiting tenure, we will be tapping a hitherto untapped source of wise—or at least wiser—people to become our leaders, for collectively they will possess a far broader and deeper knowledge of the world than the lawyers who dominate the political scene today.

Q: *To a large degree, you seem to want to give power to people who do not appear to be basically interested in power—at least, not*

*in the political arena. Why should they suddenly want to get into
politics once the tenure limitation is in force? In other words, why
should "philosophers" suddenly want to become "kings"?*

A: Today, the "philosophers," as you call them—that is, the
wiser members of society—mostly avoid the political arena because
they are repelled by the kind of politicking that goes on under the
present system, and because they feel they haven't much chance
to defeat entrenched career politicians. Under the new system,
however, they would be running against people very much like
themselves in intelligence, skill, and integrity, and so they would be
drawn to the very real opportunity to devote their talents for a few
years to the welfare of their country.

Q: *Why wouldn't opportunists enter politics in order to get
some fame so that they could return to their original businesses or
professions with a valuable public relations boost?*

A: I suppose there may be a few opportunists now and then, for
no system is foolproof. But for the most part, their political oppor-
tunism should be discouraged by their colleagues, who will be of a
higher caliber than now, and also by the greater interest that the
general public will take in scrutinizing public officials and candidates for public office once the differences between them become
more a matter of substance than style—for by that time, of course,
the apathy that we see today among the electorate should have
become a thing of the past.

Q: *Even under your system, won't there be power brokers behind the scenes to whom the officeholders will owe political favors?*

> *Whatever government is not a government of laws is a despotism, let it be called what it may.*
>
> —Daniel Webster, 1835

A: I think not. It may sound a bit idealistic, but I believe that with limited political tenure in effect, behind-the-scenes party bosses and political machines like the one formerly run by Mayor Daley in Chicago will fade away. The old methods of bribery and manipulation will be much more difficult to employ in a system in which the candidates come from successful careers outside of politics and know in advance that they will be returning to those careers after contributing their services to government for a brief and strictly limited period.

Q: *You have stated that the people give the demagogue's disease to their leaders by granting them special privileges and treating them as heroes. Do you really think that this kind of public behavior will cease simply because the politicians are limited to six or eight years in office? And if not, won't the politicians catch the demagogue's disease in the same way they do today?*

A: I suppose hero worship will always be a part of every human society. However, the higher caliber of political candidates under the new system should help see to it that far fewer officeholders succumb to the demagogue's disease; and even those who *do* fall victim to it will have only the glory without the power when that inevitable time comes for them to leave government service forever. Then they will be as harmless to society as any egotistical movie star or sports hero is today. I think that's a lot better than having the politicians exploit their glory *and* their power for thirty years or more, the way they do now.

Q: *Why are you so concerned about a phenomenon that has existed in the world for thousands of years?*

A: It's true that the demagogue's disease has existed in the world for centuries, and the planet has somehow managed to survive. However, in the last fifty years or so, tremendous changes have occurred in the world of a type and magnitude beyond anything that previous leaders had to deal with. When combined with the demagogue's disease, these changes can bring on world disaster. For example, there have been great advances in medical science and public health, but these advances have contributed in the long run to our desperate overpopulation problem, which in turn has led to massive unemployment, starvation, and other man-made catastrophes.

In a recent study called for by President Carter, fourteen federal agencies were asked to indicate what they believed would be the most pressing problems of the United States in the year 2000. A very pessimistic assessment of the world was made by those agencies in a report in which they indicated that the runaway population explosion around the world posed one of the most severe threats to this country's national security. The study predicted that deprived areas of the world could become the breeding grounds for revolution and wars against wealthy nations. The authors of the study conclude that solutions to these problems could be found by utilizing human labor in cooperative efforts, but they fear that the institutional and political barriers appear to be insurmountable. In other words, the leaders of the world are apparently unprepared to meet the challenge. The principal reason for this is

> *Power is always gradually stealing away from the many to the few.*
>
> —Samuel Johnson, 1761

not lack of intelligence but lack of will. It is more important to the leaders to maintain themselves in power than it is to solve their nations' problems.

Moreover, the irony of it is that medical science has further aggravated the situation by increasing the life spans not only of the poor and the oppressed but of the demagogues themselves. Thus we now have a world which is ruled in large part by people in their seventies and eighties. Since World War II alone, some of the more prominent leaders in their *seventies* have included: Argentina's Juan Peron, China's Chou En-lai (Zhou Enlai) and Teng Hsiao-ping (Deng Xiaoping), France's Charles de Gaulle, India's Jawaharlal Nehru, Israel's David Ben-Gurion and Golda Meir, and Russia's Joseph Stalin, Nikita Khrushchev, Leonid Brezhnev, Aleksei Kosygin, and Nikolai Podgorny. In power in their *eighties* have been such notables as: Britain's Winston Churchill, China's Mao Tse-tung (Mao Zedong), East Germany's Walter Ulbricht, West Germany's Konrad Adenauer, Ethiopia's Haile Selassie, India's Morarji Desai, Spain's Francisco Franco, Taiwan's Chiang Kai-shek, and Yugoslavia's Josip Broz Tito. The prize, however, goes to Ireland, whose Eamon de Valera was president in his *nineties.* Before the end of the century, no doubt, someone will try to be the first ruler in history to still be in office on his hundredth birthday.

But it isn't only a matter of life or death with these elderly politicians. Many of them suffer from illnesses which reduce their mental or physical abilities, or both. I concede that the leaders of countries can afford to buy the best medical attention, but that does not always guarantee a perfect mind and body. For example, one of the richest men in the world, Howard Hughes, suffered from a kidney disease which resulted in his blood not being properly cleansed by the kidney's filtering action. This caused uretic poisoning, which affected his brain and led to paranoid and other abnormal behavior. Many of the political leaders of the world are suffering from similarly severe mental and physical ailments, but normally the severity of their conditions is kept out of the press. Even in our own country, the deteriorated mental condition of President Woodrow Wilson was a well-kept secret from the American public. Politicians like that may have all of the best intentions to help their people, they may not be guilty of any corruption, but they are nevertheless doing their public a disservice by insisting that they are still qualified to hold political office. In fact, merely by taking that position, they demonstrate their incompetence and poor judgment.

Now, both the overpopulation problem and the problem of overage and enfeebled politicians are a partial result of advances in only one area: medical science. At the same time, of course, there have been advances in communications, in weapons, in automation, and in dozens of other areas which have vastly complicated the problems of the world. That is why it is so urgent for us to find ways to select leaders with wisdom rather than the gift of gab or a pretty face. It is absolutely imperative, therefore, that the people of the world be educated to see the demagogue's disease for what it is. It is simply no longer satisfactory to replace one demagogue with another. We can't afford such foolishness any longer. Unless and until career politicians are made a thing of the past, so that our leaders can devote all their energy and intelligence to searching for ways to solve the immense problems of the age, the world is going to become a spectacularly unhappy place to live in. Or more likely, to die in.

Q: *You're thinking of a nuclear war?*

> *In a change of government, the poor seldom change anything except the name of their master.*
>
> —Phaedrus, ca. 40 A.D.

A: Yes, I am. When I received secret clearance from the Department of Defense, I had an opportunity to closely study the nuclear arsenals of the major world powers—and, believe me, World War III is frightening to contemplate. Since the rulers of this planet have never been able to avoid wars, I doubt that we can avoid future wars if we continue to have the same type of power-hungry leaders that the world has seen for centuries. Thus, I want to see a totally new type of leader emerge, not just in the United States but in all countries.

Also, I feel that it won't be long before a nuclear device gets into the hands of terrorists. When that happens, there is going to be international panic, and the people of the world will clamor for law and order on a scale that could open the door to another Hitler. That is why we simply *must* start eliminating the demagogue's disease—both to alleviate the human misery around the globe and thereby reduce the discontent that breeds terrorism, and also to make it more difficult for future potential demagogues to use such crisis situations to perpetuate themselves in office.

Q: *But during a crisis of that magnitude, wouldn't the leaders simply suspend their constitutions and declare a state of emergency, much as Hitler did after the Reichstag building burned down?*

A: That would certainly be the tendency with the type of leaders we have today. But my objective, remember, is to bring in a whole new breed of political officeholders—noncareer politicians who would never consider spending a lifetime in politics, let alone establishing a thousand-year Reich.

Q: *You are obviously opposed to elderly politicians, or at least to politicians growing old in office. Yet, it has been argued by columnnist George F. Will (in the* Washington Post, *October 30, 1977) that if no one can hope to make a career of politics, then people will be apt to enter politics late in life, after establishing a "real" career, and after establishing it so well that they can afford to take a sabbatical. In other words, politicians will tend to be even older (and wealthier) than they are now. What is your response to this argument?*

A: Let me clarify, first of all, that I am in *no* way opposed to elderly politicians as such, assuming that they are in good physical and mental health. What I *am* opposed to, as you say, is politicians who grow old in office, which is another matter entirely.

As for the main part of Will's argument, I have two answers. One, in today's world, people are changing careers at *all* ages, and in unprecedented numbers. To quote from a past issue of *Life* magazine (which has since gone through a career change of its own!):

> More and more men are changing jobs today. Columbia University recently completed an experimental program just to help them change. There seem to be no limits to the leap; account executives have quit to become ministers, ministers have become engineers, and engineers have turned to raising chickens. (*Life,* June 12, 1970, p. 50.)

> *The care of human life and happiness, and*
> *not their destruction, is the first and only*
> *legitimate object of good government.*
>
> —Thomas Jefferson, 1809

The point is that people may just as easily turn to politics—and back out again after a few years—as to any other job or profession.

My second answer is that if the end of *career* politics has the effect of making people enter government service later in life than they do now—and I'm not convinced it will—that's not necessarily a bad thing. What I'm looking for from politicians, after all, is wisdom, and that's a quality most likely to be found among those of mature age and experience.

As for politicians being wealthier than they are now, I have no objection, provided they come by the money honestly. Affluence is no particular bar to competence, and is likely to prevent public servants from succumbing to bribery.

Q: *Do you believe that women are any less susceptible to the demagogue's disease than men are?*

A: I don't think we have enough data yet to prove the point one way or the other in any scientific way. For example, in the whole 200-year history of this country, there have been less than a hundred women in the House of Representatives and only twelve women senators, eleven of them widows appointed to fill out the

terms of their late husbands.* There has never been a woman
President or Vice-President here, of course, or even a Supreme
Court justice, and the entire sex has only had the vote since 1920.
Thus, up until recent times, men have made it almost impossible for
women to acquire political power in any direct way. (Even in other
countries, the exceptions in the past have occurred mostly among
hereditary monarchies.) Whether or not the women always wanted
that power is another question. However, even if we could prove
that women are naturally less susceptible than men to catching the
disease, we would still have to admit that when they do catch it,
they can be just as egotistical, self-serving, and ruthless as any man.

Looking beyond the boundaries of this country, we could
cite Indira Gandhi as a good case in point. She became so authoritarian and so cut off from the feelings of her people that her own
closest advisers were afraid to tell her how poorly she was doing in
the polls. As the saying goes, the day you become the leader of your
country is the last day you will ever hear the truth.

An even more extreme female demagogue was Chiang
Ch'ing, better known in the West as Mrs. Mao Tse-tung, who was
one of the principal architects of China's devastating Cultural Revo-

---

*According to former Congresswoman Bella Abzug, speaking on radio station KPFA in
Berkeley, California, on October 9, 1978 (a month prior to the elections of November 7), this
nation has had 87 congresswomen and eleven women senators. The 1978 elections brought
in the twelfth woman senator, Nancy Landon Kassenbaum (Rep., Kansas), who is the first
woman senator *not* to be a widow succeeding her husband. The number of current women
representatives in the House, however, dropped from eighteen to sixteen, which has been
the average delegation for the last twenty-five years. Yet, below the federal level, women
did better: They scored a net gain of 58 state legislative seats, and now hold 761, or 10.2
percent of the national total. Ten women are now serving as secretaries of state, six as state
treasurers, and six as lieutenant governors. (See "Political Scoreboard: How Women Candidates Made Out," *San Francisco Chronicle,* November 23, 1978.) According to the National
Conference of Mayors, there are now nine women mayors of American cities with at least
100,000 residents. The cities are San Francisco and San Jose, California; San Antonio and
Austin, Texas; Phoenix, Arizona; Oklahoma City, Oklahoma; St. Petersburg, Florida; Lincoln,
Nebraska; and Raleigh, North Carolina. (See Jerry Burns, "Feinstein Is Sworn In as S.F.'s New
Mayor," *San Francisco Chronicle,* December 5, 1978.) As this book went to press, Jane M.
Byrne was elected mayor of Chicago. There are also two women governors at the present
time: Dixie Lee Ray of Washington and Ella Grasso of Connecticut.

> *The government is mainly an expensive organization to regulate evildoers, and tax those who behave: government does little for fairly respectable people except annoy them.*
>
> —E. W. Howe, 1926

lution, and who is now, of course, under arrest as one of the so-called "Gang of Four."

Her counterpart on Taiwan, Madame Chiang Kai-shek, had a touch of the disease herself. Throughout her generalissimo husband's reign, this lady insisted on having silk sheets on her bed, even during her official stay at the White House.

The same kind of insensitive, extravagant behavior in the face of her countrymen's poverty is displayed today by Mrs. Marcos, wife of the president of the Philippines. This former beauty queen has been known to send her nation's jets flying around in search of fine-grained sand for her private beach and to deliver sumptuous Philippine dishes to her dinner parties when she is entertaining abroad. When she visits a school or dedicates a hospital at home, rose petals are sprinkled in her path as she approaches, and trumpets announce her entrance.

There are other examples that one could mention. For instance, both Eva and later Isabel Peron in Argentina had strong cases of the demagogue's disease, as did Madame Nhu in South Vietnam and Mrs. Sirimavo Bandaranaike, Prime Minister of Sri Lanka (Ceylon). Mrs. Tito, wife of the president of Yugoslavia, was developing a case of her own, for which she was placed under house arrest. And the list goes on and on. As these examples show us, furthermore, women can catch the disease both in their own right, if they are given the chance to wield power directly, or through their husbands (or sons, or brothers), if they are not. The extremes

appear to range from those women who have been content to be
the power or the brains behind the throne, in the manner of Lady
Macbeth, to those others who have preferred the overt glory of
their positions. Mrs. Lincoln is a good example of the latter case.
Believing that it was her duty as First Lady to be better dressed and
more elegant than any other woman in the land, she spent immense
sums of money on imported fabrics, in the process putting her
harried President husband deep into debt.

In short, then, while as a group women have had less opportunity and may have less inclination to contract the demagogue's
disease, it appears that individually they can fall just as deeply in
love with power and glory as any man can; and although female
demagogues may seem to be less brutal than their male counter-
parts, the damage they do to their countries can be just as wide and
just as deep. Thus, the need for society to protect itself against them
by limiting their political tenure is just as important as it is in the
case of men.

Q: *You've mostly been concentrating on the political consequences of the demagogue's disease. Can you indicate how the
disease might hurt a country economically?*

A: Indeed I can. One has only to think of Nigeria. In 1975, the
regime of General Yakubu Gowon, who had a full-fledged case of
the demagogue's disease, was overthrown by a military coup
largely because of an economic scandal having to do, of all things,
with cement. (See John Darnton, "Lagos Talks of a Scandal," *The
New York Times,* June 28, 1976.)* It seems that Gowon had the

---

*Copyright © 1976 by The New York Times Company. Excerpts reprinted by permission.

> *To live by one man's will became the cause of all men's misery.*
>
> —Richard Hooker, 1594

grandiose notion of rebuilding much of his country from the ground up, but he didn't really know how to go about doing it in a realistic way. Consequently, his government ordered twenty million tons of cement—sixteen million for the Ministry of Defense alone—all of it to be delivered within twelve months. What Gowon and his ministers overlooked was that at a rate of 1.6 million tons of cement per month, the shipments would amount to more than twice the unloading capacity of all of Nigeria's ports combined!

Soon there were over 420 freighters lined up as far as the eye could see outside Lagos, the capital, many of the ships being decrepit old hulks sent by their owners principally in order to collect the demurrage costs—a handsome $4,100 a day per ship. Since many of these ships had to wait for from eight months to a year to be unloaded, fortunes were being made merely for the trouble of riding at anchor. By the time the twenty million tons of cement were unloaded, the government had paid out $240 million in demurrage costs alone. And that was on top of $57 million that the government had overpaid for the cement in the first place, thanks to bribes and kickbacks to high-ranking officials. Worse yet, after sitting for long periods in moisture-ridden hulls, much of the cement had lost its binding quality and had become worthless for construction. Nevertheless, a great deal of it found its way into the hands of small contractors, and now buildings are starting to collapse all over Nigeria.

After Gowon's downfall, the new government appointed a tribunal to investigate the scandal, but it is believed that the true cost to the nation will never be known. This is because the damage went far beyond the shipping and building industries. For example, as a consequence of the ports being totally congested with the cement ships, many factories could not receive parts and so had to be closed down, the export of cocoa was brought to a standstill, and the inflation rate soared. Thus, it is thought that the economic repercussions have to run into billions of dollars—money that the people of Nigeria could hardly afford to throw away, let alone invest in crumbling buildings.

The Nigerian cement scandal is, of course, a highly dramatic case in point, but similar economic mismanagement is being carried out by incompetent demagogues throughout the Third World. I would even predict that the present rulers of Nigeria itself will soon start making equally unwise decisions as they in turn concentrate less and less on solving their nation's problems and more and more on keeping themselves in power.

Q: *Is there any way in which countries can minimize the economic chaos that always results when leaders are changed by violent upheavals?*

A: Countries where revolutions and violent coups occur need to quickly restore order, especially when various political factions are vying for the top positions. I have talked with people who were planning the overthrow of tyrants in various countries, and I know that it is extremely dangerous for opposition groups to try to work together openly *before* a coup or revolution, and that it is also immensely difficult for them to cooperate during those hectic days *after* the government has been toppled. Therefore, the country almost invariably suffers severe economic setbacks before finally achieving political stability. Frequently, stability is not achieved at

> *In all sorts of government man is made to believe himself free, and to be in chains.*
>
> —Stanislaus Leszcynski
> (King of Poland), 1763

all until the military forces take over, declare martial law, outlaw political parties, and curtail freedom of the press.

I think that normalcy could be more quickly and more equitably restored if there were immediately available a model constitution that the political factions in a country would recognize as a reasonable stopgap measure. It would at least serve until order could be restored, and the country could then patiently tailor a constitution to its own needs.

Such a stopgap constitution should contain a one-year limitation on the first post-coup leader. Following that, the country's newly adopted constitution would take over. Thus, many of the political leaders who would like to rule might exercise some restraint rather than ruthlessly rushing into the vacant position, since the first post-coup ruler would rule for the shortest time. The political parties would also show less rivalry, because instead of trying to sabotage or obstruct the first leader, they would tend to help him get the economy back on keel, knowing that at the end of the year their group might have a turn in office, inheriting a stable economy.

Most likely, the best place for such a model stopgap constitution to be drawn up would be at the United Nations. Incidentally, the UN could render another valuable service in a number of unstable countries by offering to supervise their elections and thereby remove all doubt concerning the validity of the ballot count. For generations, millions of disenfranchised people around the world have struggled for the right to vote; if they are to have faith in democracy, they are entitled to know that their elections are not a sham or a farce.

Q: *Your proposals for government reform are, of course, not the first ones ever to come along. I'd like to know what you think about some of the others, and how they may or may not be compatible with your own. For example, it has been suggested that some kind of mental and physical examination should be a prerequisite of running for political office.*

A: Perhaps there should be some minimum requirements aside from age and residency in order to qualify for the ballot, since politics is virtually the only profession in today's society that requires no training or ability. However, I would be opposed to any kind of mental examination, for, among other things, it would be exceedingly difficult to administer. Furthermore, I can envision the rash of lawsuits that would arise contending that the examination is unfair to certain groups. Many of the disadvantaged minority groups are making such arguments today against, for example, the entrance exams at universities or the bar exams in the legal profession. Their arguments would apply even more to political office, where we need leaders from all types of backgrounds and experience.

Now, if there were a test that could measure wisdom, and common sense, and honesty, and level of ambition, and depth of compassion, and *not* simply I.Q., I might be for it. Until then, we'll have to leave such matters to the judgment of the electorate.

As for physical exams, I wouldn't want to disqualify someone who had a physical disability but might otherwise make a fine leader. Yet, we don't want a repeat of the Woodrow Wilson phenomenon either, where, unbeknownst to the public, the President was totally incapacitated. Perhaps the best solution would be to require a physical examination whose results would be made public, and then let the people, rather than some board of doctors, decide with their votes whether or not they consider a political candidate healthy enough to hold office and represent their interests. Some discretionary guidelines would have to be established, of

> *To be governed is to be watched, inspected,*
> *spied upon, directed, law-ridden, regulated,*
> *penned up, indoctrinated, preached at,*
> *checked, appraised, seized, censured,*
> *commanded, by beings who have neither*
> *title, nor knowledge, nor virtue.*
>
> —P. J. Proudhon, 1849

course, so that candidates would not have their privacy unnecessarily invaded and so that potential candidates would not be discouraged from running simply because of some politically irrelevant but possibly embarrassing physical condition.

Q: *Isn't the recall election device an effective enough tool for removing incompetent or corrupt politicians?*

A: Actually, I don't believe that recall elections accomplish a great deal. In most cases, the person removed—if he *is* removed—is replaced by someone of the same caliber; so basically it's just a game of musical chairs. As more and more people realize this, voter apathy increases; and that is precisely what we have been seeing in recent years.

Q: *What about citizen pressure groups and committees to bring about reform?*

A: In most cases, such groups are formed to redress one particular wrong, rather than to remove one or more demagogues from office. The groups are typically disorganized and nearsighted, lack continued financing, and so are frequently short-lived. They may correct the wrong that caused them anguish in the first place, but the demagogues continue   office as always.

Q: *What you say is not true of such major national organizations as Common Cause. They not only seek to redress particular wrongs, but they also devote a great deal of time and money to weeding out many of the politicians that you're complaining about.*

A: It's true that a number of groups, including Common Cause, do achieve results, and I particularly applaud Common Cause's attempts to educate its members about the great advantages that incumbents have over their opponents when running for reelection. It's known, for instance, that merely being an incumbent is worth approximately a million dollars worth of free publicity and services to a senator, and nearly half that much to the average congressman. Nevertheless, when it comes down to specifics, groups like Common Cause still tend to go in earnest after only the worst and most obvious offenders, while I'm more interested in making changes across the board.

For example, Common Cause studies the records of politicians in great detail, and when it appears that one of them is dishonest or incompetent, Common Cause starts to urge that person's removal. But success is not always immediate: it may take years to dislodge an unfit professional politician. More likely than not, that politician, if unseated from a congressional seat, will somehow get himself elected to a position in state politics.

I want to make the removal process regular and automatic. Why should society have to wait until the demagogue's disease is so obvious that the politician has to be forcibly removed from office?

> *The thirst for glory is an epidemic which
> robs a people of their judgment, seduces their
> vanity, cheats them of their interests, and
> corrupts their consciences.*
>
> —W. G. Sumner, 1899

We need a system that prevents officeholders from contracting the disease in the first place. It's a case of an ounce of prevention being worth a pound of cure.

Q: *As an outgrowth of Watergate and the Korean bribes of congressmen, aren't the legislators themselves bringing about reform by introducing codes of ethics and committee reorganizations that may make for better leadership?*

A: I don't see how those things will appreciably change the politicians as political animals. Their first principle will still be to get themselves reelected. Until *that* temptation is removed, we will never get the best people in the job, let alone get the best efforts from the more or less mediocre talents who are there now.

Q: *You seem to be blaming all of the nation's troubles on its political leaders. But aren't many of today's problems out of their control—perhaps even out of human control? For example, our present energy resources are eventually going to be used up, no matter who is in political office.*

A: It's true that some problems are beyond political or even human control, and I certainly wouldn't want to give the impression that I'm blaming the weather, or earthquakes, or plane crashes, or any other natural or manmade catastrophes on Congress or the White House. Our *responses* to those problems, however, are not out of our control—or, at least, shouldn't and needn't be—and that's where the excellence of our leadership comes in.

Now, you've mentioned energy resources, and that brings me to the point that some of our problems are caused by the leaders of *other* countries. The United States certainly has no monopoly when it comes to demagogues, so it is my ultimate hope that career politicians will be driven into extinction on a worldwide basis. Only when the demagogue's disease is eliminated in *all* lands will we be totally immune to it here.

Q: *All right, let's turn our attention to foreign countries. How would your proposal to limit tenure affect a country like Great Britain, where the government can be changed much more quickly than in the United States, and where members of Parliament tend to vote along party lines?*

A: This may come as something of a surprise to you, but in many ways, in my opinion, the British are ahead of us in combating the demagogue's disease. First of all, they've separated the power and the glory at the highest level of government by giving the power to the Prime Minister and the glory to the Crown. Furthermore, given the nation's aristocratic background, their politicians seem on the whole to be better educated and more articulate than ours. At the same time, incidentally, they're paid a great deal less than ours; yet there seem to be fewer political scandals over there, and the ones they do have usually have more to do with sex than with money.

> *I do not wish to be king because that is to be
> tempted to cruelty.*
>
> —Publius Syrus, ca. 43 B.C.

Having said all this, I still believe there's room for limited political tenure in Britain. The members of the House of Lords have tenure for life, and perhaps that's alright, given their very limited powers. But members of the House of Commons and politicians at other levels should have their tenures limited in the same way that I would like to see political service limited in this country. I wouldn't care to get too specific about the number of years that would work best over there, for that's something for the British to work out among themselves. Nevertheless, the principle remains basically the same, and for most of the same reasons that I've already given in respect to the United States.

Now, as for your point about how the government in Britain can be changed more quickly than in the United States: That's because (1) the Prime Minister is given his office by his party rather than by the electorate, and because (2) national elections can be called at almost any time. Neither of those principles, fortunately or unfortunately, could be exported to the United States, because the tradition of having all the people vote for the President is too deeply ingrained, and because we're not a homogeneous and stable enough society to be able to handle elections every time we have a crisis. Under the British system, on the one hand, a Nixon would have been removed from office right at the start of the Watergate disclosures, and that's certainly good. But, on the other hand, we would probably go the way of Italy, with governments coming in and going out every few months. That kind of revolving-door tenure is too brief even for me.

As for party-line discipline: Again, it works well for the British, who divide politically along more or less ideological lines; but it would not thrive over here, where the political divisions are more between diverse interest groups than ideologies. I can't say that I'm totally happy with this answer, because party-line discipline tends to reduce the power and the glory of the individual politician, and thus tends to suppress the demagogue's disease; but it does this in a way that would not be accepted in this country, so there's no point in advocating it.

Q: *You mentioned Italy just now and its revolving-door governments. Since rapid political turnover is certainly the case there, do you think there's any need to formally limit political tenure when the real problem is to get a little more stability into the situation so that the politicians can stay around long enough to have some effect? In other words, don't you think that Italy provides a rather poor environment for the demagogue's disease these days, and that therefore the solutions to its problems will have to come from other directions?*

A: Don't confuse revolving-door governments in Italy with revolving-door politicians. While the titles may change, the faces remain more or less the same. It's only a matter of bringing a few more Socialists into the coalition, or of making a few more concessions to the Communists, but basically it boils down to just one more version of adult musical chairs. In short, thirty years after Mussolini, Italy is no more immune to the demagogue's disease than any other country in the world, and it would profit as much as any from shaking the dead wood out of its political system by making career politicians obsolete.

Q: *How would your proposal stop a madman like Hitler? It's very unlikely, first of all, that such a fanatical leader would volun-*

> Government is an association of men who do
> violence to the rest of us.
>
> —Leo Tolstoy, 1893

*tarily obey even a constitutional requirement to step down. Fur-
thermore, by the time Hitler had been in office for eight years,
which you propose as the absolute limit in the United States, he had
had more than enough time to turn much of the world into a
shambles.*

A: It's too late, of course, for my proposal to stop Adolf Hitler
from ascending to power in 1933, but I have high hopes that it will
stop the potential Hitlers of the 1980s and beyond. The world is
changing very quickly, and in less than a generation we may well
see limited political tenure accepted more or less universally. At
that point, any national leader who tried to violate the tenure
limitation of his country would instantly invite political, economic,
and, if necessary, military intervention from the international community at large. If that sounds farfetched, bear in mind that we
have already applied political and economic pressure on governments (such as those in Rhodesia, South Africa, and Uganda under
Amin) whose oppression has been directed principally against their
own people.

　　As for eight years being more than enough time to plunge
the world into chaos, that's quite true. Remember, however, that
a demagogue like Hitler was not *planning* to be around for only
eight years. In fact, he intended to remain in power for life, and
claimed that he was building an empire which would last for a
thousand years.

　　Now, if all leaders of the world were aware that the international community would come to the rescue of any nation whose

leader violated his country's constitutional limitation on tenure, that knowledge alone would be an inhibiting factor in the leaders' conduct. It is precisely because the leaders think there is *no* limitation on how long they can remain in power that they are uninhibited in their use of oppression.

Q: *You seem to be forgetting that Hitler rode in on a wave of mass hysteria, the likes of which could be repeated in many places around the world today were there to be, say, a deep economic depression, or a prolonged famine, or a series of natural catastrophes, or terrorists exploding atomic bombs. Under such conditions, wouldn't the people look for a forceful—possibly even a fanatical—leader to create order out of the chaos? And for being able to do that, wouldn't his reward be the people's toleration of his permanent stay in office?*

A: It's true that Hitler came to power on a theme of law and order, and it's also true that such a grotesque phenomenon as the Third Reich could probably be repeated today, given the type of catastrophes you mention. But it is precisely my point that with better government we can and must *prevent* such catastrophes— at least the kind that are produced by human forces. Earthquakes or floods or tornadoes or hurricanes or volcanic eruptions don't usually cause political upheavals. But depressions and famines, which are manmade—or, at least, which are humanly preventable —do.

The one possible exception to what I'm saying, and one that is almost too horrible to contemplate, is the explosion of atomic bombs by political terrorists. In that case, so much destruction could be caused by so few people that the situation might easily get out of hand. Of course, *no* political system is going to prevent some psychopath from blowing up a city, but if we can get on with solving

> *You can always get the truth from an
> American statesman after he has turned
> seventy, or given up all hope of the
> Presidency.*
>
> —Wendell Phillips, 1860

the problems of the world, we might just possibly reduce his incentive to do so.

Q: *Why would nations exert political or economic pressure, let alone go to war, against a tyrant who only oppresses his own people?*

A: As I indicated earlier, the countries of the world are becoming increasingly interdependent every day. Thus, when the people of one country are oppressed, to some degree we are all oppressed, and we are all responsible for that oppression if we do nothing to stop it. Furthermore, sooner or later most tyrants outgrow their own people and look for wider territories to conquer—or perhaps they manufacture external threats to consolidate their domestic power. In any case, we all have a moral responsibility to remove such demagogues wherever they may be, and, far from being an idle dream, the United States has already worked in this direction by, for example, boycotting Uganda's coffee exports in an effort to topple Idi Amin's despotic and corrupt regime.

Q: *What are your views on contemporary France and West Germany in terms of the demagogue's disease?*

A: Postwar France and West Germany have both had their share of demagogues—that is, leaders infatuated with power and glory. At the highest level, Germany had Konrad Adenauer, who practically had to be pried from office with a crowbar—and by his own party, since he could not tolerate having anyone around him who showed political promise, and therefore the Christian Democrats were being debilitated from within.

In France, of course, there was Charles de Gaulle, whose love of glory, if not of power, is scarcely rivaled in this or any other century—aside, of course, from the Fascist and Nazi madmen. To find parallels in French history, one would have to go back to Charlemagne, Louis XIV, and Napoleon.

However, I don't want to dwell overly long on particular personalities, for there are some good things to be said for the West German and French systems from the perspective of the demagogue's disease. For example, in West Germany they've divided the power and the glory between a Prime Minister and a President respectively, and this pattern prevails in most of the Western democracies that no longer have reigning monarchs. Since de Gaulle, of course, France has had a strong presidential office, with the Prime Minister taking second place, and this has been useful in countering the revolving-door syndrome that used to prevail there in the Italian manner.

Aside from these generalizations, however, and without repeating everything I've already said in respect to the United States, Britain, and Italy, I see no reason to doubt that France, West Germany, Japan, Canada, Australia, and all the other democracies of the world would benefit enormously from putting the demagogue's disease on the same shelf as polio, smallpox, and the Black Plague.

Q: *Your proposal has a chance of being voted in someday in the democracies. But what chance does it have in the Communist coun-*

> *We favor a single presidential term, and to
> that end urge the adoption of an amendment
> to the Constitution making the President of
> the United States ineligible for reelection,
> and we pledge the candidate of this
> convention to this principle.*
>
> —Democratic National Platform, 1912

tries, where the leaders have never shown any disposition to relinquish power?

A: The Communist countries may well be the last ones to jump on the bandwagon, and they may do so in a manner and with a style very different from ours; but it is my firm belief that do it they will. When limitation on political tenure begins to catch on in various countries around the world, and when the obvious benefits of this become apparent for all to see, there will be internal pressure within the Communist countries to follow suit.

After all, there is nothing in the proposal that could in any way be interpreted as anti-Communist. The idea cuts across all political systems in a positive way, just as the demagogue's disease cuts across all political systems in a negative way.

It's true that the Soviet system, below the topmost level, allows its politicians less *glory* than most, since the Russians and their Eastern European colleagues have a penchant for keeping their political decisions impersonal and anonymous; but the price for operating in this way is that the politicians receive a proportionately greater share of *power* than is true, say, in the West. Since the death of Stalin, of course—or more accurately, since Khrushchev's de-Stalinization program in the fifties—the Communists have officially condemned the so-called cult of personality; and they have always expressed, even if they haven't always followed, the view that no individual is indispensable. It is only a short step from there to the idea that no politician should serve for more than a limited period.* Thus, there are no significant theoretical obstacles to my idea being accepted by Communist doctrine. The major practical obstacle—the raw human lust for power and glory—will be harder to overcome, but the younger generations will take up the task sooner than you think.

Q: *What about countries like Saudi Arabia and Kuwait, where there are absolute monarchs and little or no attempt at democracy? Do you expect such monarchs to step down voluntarily at some point and hand over their power to the people?*

A   Not at all. More likely, the people—or the military—will take the power by force. There is absolutely no reason to assume that those monarchies are going to last forever. In Iran, for example, the powerful Shah proved to be no more permanent a fixture than was King Farouk in Egypt or Emperor Haile Selassie in Ethiopia.

       Saudi Arabia and Kuwait, in fact, are both examples of countries in which the new oil wealth is simultaneously pulling them in two contradictory directions. On the one hand, they are seeking technical modernization; but on the other hand, the rulers' power base requires that the people remain relatively backward. The problem is, if you want a modern economy, you need to educate scientists, engineers, military experts, doctors, lawyers, teachers, and other people who are not going to be content to sit back and let an absolute monarch run the country as his private medieval

---

*A few weeks after I made this statement, reports started to come out of China that Mao Tse-tung's image was going through a major revision. He was a great man in his earlier years, said the wall posters, but in his later years, influenced by the "Gang of Four," he made many mistakes. This criticism is, of course, totally consistent with what I have been saying about political leaders in general. Unfortunately, people tend to focus on particular leaders and overlook the general principle that applies to all of them.

> *Few politicians die, and none resign.*
>
> —Thomas Jefferson, 1801

fiefdom. So, in a way, the present rulers of those countries are digging their own graves.

The question then becomes: What can be done about those countries after they are no longer absolute monarchies? Most likely, they will become military dictatorships, and then the same kind of internal pressure will build up in them as I have already described for the Communist countries. Eventually, even if their political structures remain relatively authoritarian, the need for rotating political leaders will become apparent, and the countries will be reformed accordingly.

Q: *Don't some dictators benefit their nations by bringing stability and efficiency to government?*

A: Yes, sometimes they do. Often they appoint very capable ministers; and their military officers, many of whom have studied abroad, can be highly competent and efficient administrators. In fact, the dictators themselves can be extremely qualified. Many, dedicated to a vision of what is best for their countries, have excellent long-range developmental plans and can carry them along well for a few years.

What the dictators tend to overlook, however, are their equally patriotic and qualified countrymen yearning for an active role in shaping their nations' future. When such people are excluded from power, friction is inevitable. It may result in protests, followed by revolt, which finally destroys much of what the dictator had built. So what good are those few years of efficiency if they end in violent upheaval and economic chaos?

Q: *What about the poor Third World countries of Asia, Africa, and Latin America, which have no oil income to force modernization upon them, and which are in fact in desperate financial straits? What will induce such countries to adopt your proposals?*

A: As a matter of fact, it was thinking about the Third World countries that led me to the idea of the demagogue's disease and its cure in the first place, for it is in just those countries that the disease is most rampant. Leaders like Idi Amin in Uganda, "Baby Doc" Duvalier in Haiti, Anastasio Somoza in Nicaragua, Jean Bedel Bokassa in the Central African Empire, and Park Chung Hee in South Korea are walking examples of the disease, some to the point of caricature.

However, improbable as this may sound, I have a feeling that the Third World countries may actually be the first to adopt my proposal, for they are continually experiencing coups and drafting new constitutions, and my idea would allow them to retain their relatively rapid turnover of political personnel, but in an orderly fashion and without bloodshed or violence. It's only a matter of time before the influential people in those countries—the businessmen, the military, and the intelligentsia—as well as the ordinary people, see that replacing one demagogue with another is tragically self-defeating. The solution lies in immunizing their political institutions from the demagogue's disease by strictly limiting political tenure at all levels. As a matter of fact, it's a golden opportunity for the Third World to become the First World in the area of political progress.

Epilogue

Whatever else one might say about the present state of the world, it must be admitted that, short of a nuclear war, the planet could hardly be much worse off than it is today. This lamentable state of affairs is, I believe, directly attributable to the low quality of our political leadership: the old system of career politics simply isn't working anymore.

Since tenure limitation might very well bring on dramatic improvements in the world's health, I feel very strongly that we should give it a chance. If it doesn't work we lose nothing, for we can always revert to the inefficient system we have now. I believe, however, that several countries will implement tenure limitation within the next few years and that it will prove highly successful. When it does, other nations will follow.

If by some chance the world should not adopt this idea in the near future, there is an excellent possibility that it will do so after World War III. I am quite certain that it will do so after World War IV. Yet, it is my fervent prayer that our recovery from the ravages of the demagogue's disease can be accomplished without war. If this book can make even the slightest contribution to that recovery, it will have served its purpose. As the Chinese say, a journey of a thousand miles begins with the first step.

Appendix A

During the 1960s and 1970s, there were attempts (some successful, some not) to overthrow governments of 81 nations by means of armed revolts, assassinations, coups, or revolutions. The nations in which these attempts occurred are listed below:

Afghanistan
Algeria
Angola
Argentina
Bangladesh
Benin
Bolivia
Brazil
Burma
Burundi
Cambodia
Central African Empire
Chad
Chile
Congo
Cuba
Cyprus
Dominican Republic
Ecuador
El Salvador
Ethiopia

Gabon
Ghana
Greece
Grenada
Guatemala
Guinea
Guyana
Haiti
Honduras
Indonesia
Iran
Iraq
Ireland, Northern
Italy
Ivory Coast
Kenya
Korea, South
Laos
Lebanon
Lesotho
Libya

Madagascar	Seychelles
Malaysia	Sierra Leone
Maldives	Somalia
Mali	South Africa
Mauritania	Spain
Morocco	Sri Lanka
Mozambique	Sudan
Nicaragua	Syria
Niger	Thailand
Nigeria	Togo
Oman	Tunisia
Pakistan	Turkey
Panama	Uganda
Paraguay	Upper Volta
Peru	Venezuela
Philippines	Vietnam
Portugal	Yemen
Rhodesia (Zimbabwe)	Yemen (Southern)
Rwanda	Zaire
Saudi Arabia	

Appendix B

[EXCERPTS FROM SENATE HEARING ON CONGRESSIONAL TENURE]

TUESDAY, MARCH 14, 1978

U.S. Senate,
Subcommittee on the Constitution
of the Committee on the Judiciary, Washington, D.C.

STATEMENT OF HON. DENNIS DECONCINI, DEMOCRATIC SENATOR FROM
THE STATE OF ARIZONA

". . . Some would argue that American voters still have a choice; they can, if they so desire, 'throw the rascal out.' My contention is that the powers of incumbency are so great that the voter is really offered only the illusion of choice. It has been estimated that the value of being the incumbent in a House race is worth roughly $500,000. While it is more difficult to calculate such a figure for the Senate because each Senator's allowance varies according to the size of his State, a figure on the average of $1 million would not seem to be far off. Furthermore, political interest groups funnel most of their campaign contributions to incumbents, thereby reinforcing their already substantial advantages. . . .

"Our constituents complain—and we complain—about the Federal bureaucracy. It is entrenched. It is unresponsive. It is practically immune to change. We often ask of these professional civil servants whether they exist to serve us, or we them? At the same time that we launch these verbal assaults, we are anxious to perpetuate an entrenched, institutional legislature. What is the difference between a professional bureaucracy and a professionalized legislature? . . ."

TESTIMONY OF HON. JOHN C. DANFORTH, REPUBLICAN SENATOR FROM
THE STATE OF MISSOURI

". . . The first point is that the purpose of the amendments is to try to move more in the direction of attracting citizen legislators in Congress, people who view themselves as private citizens on leave to their Government—as opposed to professional politicians who leave the districts or the States in which they have lived their lives and set up shop in Washington to stay as long as they possibly can. . . .

"The second point that we have been making repeatedly is this: When you are constantly looking toward the next election, and when that is foremost in your mind, there is a very human tendency to do almost anything to keep yourself in office, to get yourself reelected. Let's face it, being in the U.S. Senate is a very satisfying job. It is a job which is very interesting. You have a good staff to help you do the job. We have various emoluments of office, some of which take the form of salaries. Others take the form of gymnasiums and elevators that are marked 'Senators Only,' and the like. It is only human nature to want to stay in that kind of setting. Where do you go after being a U.S. Senator?

"So, constantly, supplicants come to Washington to ask us to do things for them. The tendency is to say 'yes' because a politician's bread and butter is to say 'yes.' Maybe we've been saying 'yes' too often and 'no' too seldom. Maybe we have been too anxious to say anything, and do anything, and promise anything, in order to win the next election. Maybe this is the reason that the Federal budget is now approaching half a trillion dollars. Maybe this is the reason the Government continues to expand like Topsy in an effort to satisfy all of the demands made on us. . . ."

TESTIMONY OF HON. S. I. HAYAKAWA, REPUBLICAN SENATOR FROM THE STATE OF CALIFORNIA

". . . Come January following every election year, newly elected Representatives travel to Washington, D.C., and settle in. Most bring families. They send their children to the local schools; they join the local churches and the local social clubs; and they make friends with other Representatives and Government people.

"When we return to our constituents during the special recesses set aside for the purposes of returning to our communities, we are too often greeted as emissaries from Washington, rather than as members of the local community from which we were elected. This is to be expected. We come here fresh from the farm, from business, from the academic world, and are given the responsibility for millions and billions of dollars. We are invited to the White House. We are given beautiful offices and large staffs to put in them. We can park anywhere we want because of our special license plates. People say, 'Yes sir,' and jump when we snap our fingers. We hobnob with the diplomats, news media, presidents, and kings—people we would rarely have the opportunity to meet if we were not wearing the special insignia and clothing of a legislator. All too often we forget that we are farmers, teachers, and businessmen, not Greek gods.

"This atmosphere is so intoxicating that after we are defeated, or after our term of office has expired, some people just cannot go back home to Idaho, or Minnesota, or California, or Rhode Island. They stay here, and stay here, and stay here with jobs as lobbyists because they get the intoxication—they get the sense that they belong here after they have served their terms, rather than in North Dakota or Rhode Island, or wherever they came from.

"Constitutional limits are placed on the number of terms a President may serve so that Presidential authority will not reside too long in the hands of one man. I don't know why the same logic does not apply to Senators and Congressmen. We can apply the concept of curtailing power by limiting time in office to assure that legislative authority will not reside too long in the hands of too few people. . . ."

TESTIMONY OF HON. THOMAS B. CURTIS, FORMER REPUBLICAN
REPRESENTATIVE IN CONGRESS FROM THE STATE OF MISSOURI AND
FORMER CHAIRMAN OF THE FEDERAL ELECTION COMMISSION

". . . Added to all this, the national news media, particularly since the advent of television, radio, national news syndicates, national magazines, today stands between the representative and his constituency in reporting back to them on what is transpiring in the legislative mill. What is reported becomes more important than what has occurred. Gaining the good will of the national news media has become an overriding factor in Federal political life, to the extent that those who control the reporting mechanisms have acquired vast political power.

"Two, the Congress is the only sizable institution in our society which is not annually audited by outside auditors and the audits made public. This secrecy invites corruption and what is equally sinister, blackmail. Selective concealment and selective disclosure is a powerful force which constant and timely full disclosure nullifies. I am talking about symptoms. Symptoms that are allowed to grow to where the whole institution, in my judgment, is corrupted. . . .

"I mention one symptom, in the budget area. The real affirmative job of the Congress is expenditures. It is not taxation and it is not monetary policy; those should be as neutral as possible. But expenditures policies should be affirmative. But here the Congress has totally lost control—I repeat—totally lost control of expenditures. This recent budget reform isn't going to do the job.

"When Congress calls items in the budget, uncontrollable items, this is pushing responsibility under the rug. Of course Congress can control every single item in the budget. . . .

"The congressmen are amply paid. In fact, their salaries are too high for part-time employees. They need the economic security of having a job, a trade, a profession, a farm or business to fall back upon if they are defeated for reelection. This gives them independence. They should always be willing to court defeat for voting and speaking their views. This independence they can have if the part-time nature of their role is kept clearly in the public's mind. Above all, they can remain a part of the communities they seek to represent and speak for them, and not become denizens of Washington, D.C., too available to the pressures and mores of the artificial community which is so overrepresented in our government today."

* * *

Thursday, March 16, 1978

TESTIMONY OF HON. BERKLEY BEDELL, DEMOCRATIC REPRESENTATIVE
IN CONGRESS FROM THE STATE OF IOWA

". . . A steady influx of new people fresh from the cities, towns, and farms of America, who will approach issues and problems with new perspectives and vitality, would be a strong antidote to congressional lethargy. It would, in my view, serve to enhance the ability of the Congress to deal with contemporary problems. . . .

"Before leaving this subject, I would like to comment briefly on the need for a 4-year House term. Such a provision is designed to allow Members of the House to devote greater time and energy to their primary task of legislating. Under the current practice of biennial elections, Congressmen spend a great deal of time and money running for office. I think that this preoccupation with one's reelection prospects constitutes a disruptive force in policymaking and places an unhealthy burden on the electoral process...."

TESTIMONY OF HON. TOBY MOFFETT, DEMOCRATIC REPRESENTATIVE IN
CONGRESS FROM THE STATE OF CONNECTICUT

"... As you no doubt realize, the issue of limiting terms is hardly a new notion. To say that it is an 'idea whose time has come' would be a gross understatement of the facts. Term limitation is an idea whose time is long overdue....

"Legislators lose that crucial 'sense of urgency' that led them to run for office in the first place. They become insulated against the everyday woes of citizens. Human misery, starvation, deprivation, environmental decay, potential nuclear destruction: These become mere words, not genuine conditions....

"Contrary to popular belief—as fostered in the media—the so-called Watergate Class of 1974, of which I am a member, did not destroy the seniority system in the House. Seniority, as we all know, is alive and well, along with its attendant fiefdoms, dominance over legislative priorities, and control over staff and funding in committees. One Senator or one Representative can tie up legislation for months—can, in fact, singlehandedly kill proposals which a majority of his or her committee may favor. A limit on terms would help restrict certain abuses in the committee process....

"It has been suggested that we need to develop 'the right formula' to attract good people into government. Personally, I do not adhere to that view—We already have many, many good people, both in the House and the Senate. What concerns me is what transpires *after* they arrive in Washington. It is the overall process to which we must direct our attention...."

TESTIMONY OF HON. ROBERT W. KASTEN, JR., REPUBLICAN
REPRESENTATIVE IN CONGRESS FROM THE STATE OF WISCONSIN

"... I think that you can argue, although this panel might not be representative, that there were an awful lot of people elected in 1974 and 1976 who could become, or maybe even are, career politicians. These are people who are relatively younger but who were preparing themselves for one job and that was to run for office and to win elections. They wanted to do well in the media, and to know how to use the 6 o'clock and 10 o'clock news, and to know how to talk in 30- and 45-second segments.

"This group of people could very easily be the next problem. Right now we are running against Congress because that is one way to get elected. With the computers and all the other tools that are at our disposal, I think there is a strong argument that could be made that this group of people could be more entrenched than the group we have been in the process of replacing. . . ."

PREPARED STATEMENT OF HON. MARK O. HATFIELD, REPUBLICAN SENATOR FROM THE STATE OF OREGON

". . . The Congress is only now entering the 20th Century and becoming capable of dealing with contemporary problems. The lack of new faces, the concentration of power and the seniority system have held the institution back from providing services, equipment and information necessary for the accomplishment of its tasks.

"New people and new ideas are always needed. One way to assure that these people and ideas enter the national legislative area is to put a limit on service, thereby providing the turnover to assure such opportunities. This change would benefit the many able men and women already serving in one of the two Houses of Congress as well. The sabbatical concept has long been employed by colleges and universities who recognize the healthy aspects of allowing, or even forcing, personnel to refresh their knowledge and not to become insular. Many industries are beginning to employ the same reasoning and are sending their personnel on sabbaticals that take them abroad or into government or back to school. The healthy effects of an enforced sabbatical for Members of Congress would surely be reflected in a better awareness of their constituencies and a better awareness of their world. Washington, D.C. is, after all, a company town and the company is the Federal Government. It is in the interests of keeping the Government responsive to the people that we should require Members of Congress to reacquaint themselves with their State, their District and their constituents, and to be removed periodically from the daily pressures of congressional life, gaining new perspectives and ideas.

"Limitation of tenure produces an opportunity for public service, pure and simple. We are all too well aware that the demands on a Senator or Representative are enormous—there is never enough time. Committee meetings, votes and hearings—the business of Congress—suffer most. In all candor, much of the congressional day is spent pursuing those tasks essential to reelection—heavy concentration on mail, press activities, meeting lobbyists and constituents, and speaking before numerous groups on every imaginable subject. Of course, these are immensely important tasks. Yet, the pressures of perpetual reelection push them to unrealistic lengths. Unfortunately, what often suffers is the time devoted to the actual legislative process. One solution is to limit tenure and thereby assure that a portion of the legislative body would be relatively free from the demands of reelection to concentrate on legislative activity. . . ."

PREPARED STATEMENT BY HON. ELWOOD H. HILLIS, REPUBLICAN
REPRESENTATIVE IN CONGRESS FROM THE STATE OF INDIANA

". . . Professional staffs, office expenses, franking privileges, and media attention all help an incumbent campaign, to some degree, 365 days a year, every year. As incumbents become safer or more entrenched in their jobs, the less likely they are to worry about whether they are truly representing the opinions of their constituents. . . .

"As anyone who has held a public office for any length of time knows, it is a way of life that is difficult to give up. Holding public office is a great honor and is always very interesting. The fast pace, the excitement of being a part of the action, the attention and privileges associated with the job, and the personal fulfillment one experiences in holding public office, all add to the difficulties of leaving it. However, whenever a Member of Congress or a Senator is unable, without any hesitation or regret, to turn his back and walk away from the job in order to allow others an opportunity to bring their ideas, it is time he or she be replaced. None of us who serve in Congress is blessed with any special wisdom or knowledge which separates us from the crowds. There will always be new and talented people ready to replace each of us. . . ."

PREPARED STATEMENT BY HON. MALCOLM WALLOP, REPUBLICAN
SENATOR FROM THE STATE OF WYOMING

". . . With unlimited congressional terms, we have risked breeding a body of professional politicians manipulating a seniority system that is at times undemocratic and always unequally representative. In all probability, only a constitutional limit on terms can bring the recurring change necessary to instill new faces and new ideas in a stagnant system. Self-restraint, such as our early presidents subscribed to, has not worked. . . ."

EXCERPT FROM INTERVIEW WITH HON. JOHN C. DANFORTH,
REPUBLICAN SENATOR FROM THE STATE OF MISSOURI

(Submitted into the record from U.S. News & World Report, *November 14, 1977)*

Q: *What are the prospects for your proposal?*

A: It's not going to get anywhere unless there's a public outcry for it. The pressure is going to have to come from the people. . . .

Appendix C

[EXCERPTS FROM CONGRESSIONAL HEARING ON ONE SIX-YEAR PRESIDENTIAL TERM]

WEDNESDAY, SEPTEMBER 26, 1973

House of Representatives
Subcommittee on Crime
of the Committee on the Judiciary,
Washington, D.C.

STATEMENT BY HON. E. (KIKA) DE LA GARZA, DEMOCRATIC
REPRESENTATIVE IN CONGRESS FROM THE STATE OF TEXAS

". . . It is a striking fact that the only constitutional restrictions on qualifying for the biggest job in the world is that the President must be a U.S. citizen not below the age of thirty-five years. Are these sufficient nowadays? Should we expect more? What standards are necessary for a person actually to qualify for being President of the United States? . . ."

TESTIMONY OF HON. CHARLES E. CHAMBERLAIN, REPUBLICAN
REPRESENTATIVE IN CONGRESS FROM THE STATE OF MICHIGAN

". . . The problem has been well stated by former Presidential assistant Jack Valenti, who has written—and I believe this may be a quote that was alluded to earlier:

" 'The man who holds that office has to deal with problems so monstrous, so disruptive, so resistant to permanent solution that the reelection process is no longer suitable. The President cannot be allowed to be diverted from his hard duties and even harder decisions by the so-called normalcies of politics and reelection.'

"While the demands on the modern Presidency make the need for a change in election procedure that much more pressing, interest in a 6-year term for the Chief Executive actually dates back to the early days of our Republic. Considerable discussion of a 6-year term took place at the Constitutional Convention in 1787, and well over a hundred amendments

212

have been offered to achieve that purpose since the Constitution became operative. . . .

"But I feel that we have arrived at that point in the history of our country with all of our technological advances, with our atomic bombs and instant communication and satellites and everything else, when we should minimize the political activities of our President after he has taken his oath of office, and have him motivated by just two basic concerns: (1) to do the best job he can as President and find his place in history, and (2) to make his peace with his maker and not have to be concerned about 'how will I get reelected. . . . ' "

STATEMENT OF HON. ALBERT H. QUIE, REPUBLICAN REPRESENTATIVE IN CONGRESS FROM THE STATE OF MINNESOTA

". . . A single six-year term would remove some of the inherent weaknesses in the present system. With all of the stress on the office, it is intolerable that a President eager to run for a second term must begin campaigning in the first. Yet this is the situation. Reelection places yet another burden on a President whose time should be occupied with guiding the Ship of State, executing its laws, and steering legislation through Congress. Clearly, the Chief Executive should not be forced to abandon worthwhile proposals during the last two years to campaign for another four.

"Outside his election circle he is saddled with requests by incumbents and newcomers, all of whom have their say. Members of Congress obsessed with Oval Office aspirations seek to destroy his reelection chances. As a consequence, White House decisions are made not for the benefit of the Nation, but for the benefit of survival. Inside his election circle, he is surrounded by administrative personnel whose positions of trust depend upon the President's survival; persons whose main duties during election time are to 'sell' the President, not to serve him. . . ."

STATEMENT OF HON. MIKE MANSFIELD, DEMOCRATIC SENATOR FROM THE STATE OF MONTANA

". . . What of the arguments against this proposition? One argument goes that when a President is elected for a single term of six years, he immediately becomes a lame duck. But the same is true today as soon as a President has been reelected to a second term—the 22nd Amendment saw to that. And upon examination it is really no argument at all.

"Lameness is by no means inherent in a single term. It relates to the strength and quality of the man holding the office.

"If a President becomes a lame duck, it is not because of any inhibitions imposed by a single term. An unlimited number of terms would not sustain such a man.

"On the other hand, a six-year President who rises to his responsibilities will have sufficient time to organize an effective and successful administration.

"Six years is not the magic number, to be sure; five or seven years will do just as well. But, conversely, six years is long enough for one man to endure in a position filled with the pressures and tensions, the worries and responsibilities of the Presidency. . . ."

Appendix D

[EXCERPTS FROM SENATE HEARING ON ONE SIX-YEAR PRESIDENTIAL TERM]

THURSDAY, OCTOBER 28, 1971

U.S. Senate,
Subcommittee on Constitutional Amendments
of the Committee on the Judiciary,
Washington, D.C.

STATEMENT OF HON. GEORGE D. AIKEN, REPUBLICAN SENATOR FROM
THE STATE OF VERMONT

". . . When a new President is inaugurated, he is usually permitted to have a wonderful time for the first 2 or 3 months and then the attacks begin and grow with intensity as the time for another national election draws nearer. He is not only subject to attack from the party which is out of the White House, but also from innumerable members of his own party who didn't get what they thought they were going to get when they supported him for President.

"He is required to spend more and more time defending himself against these attacks, some of which may be justified but more of which are aimed at defeating him should he be a candidate for reelection.

"The 6-year term will not remove 'politics' from the Office of the Presidency.

"What it will do is to remove to a great extent the President's worry over his own personal political standing and allow him to make decisions free from the temptation of political expediency. . . ."

* * *

FRIDAY, OCTOBER 29, 1971

JACK VALENTI, FORMER WHITE HOUSE AIDE, ARGUES THAT THE
PRESIDENT SHOULD SERVE LONGER AND BE INELIGIBLE FOR
REELECTION

(Submitted into the record from the Saturday Review, *August 3, 1968)*

". . . President Johnson once remarked to a meeting of his staff that, in the Presidency in this modern age, to be 99 and 55/100 per cent right was not enough. Perfection was not a goal to be sought; it was mandatory. In point of fact, the nation must regard as a national asset future Presidents' brutal insistence on perfection. Thus, it becomes rational and reasonable to strip the Presidency of all fat, to take from it that which is not essential to make more purposeful that which is. The reelection process becomes blubber, a national bloat weighing down on the efficiency of the Presidency. . . .

"The point is that the six-year term (or some stated one-term length) is not so radical. Jefferson originally favored a Presidential term of seven years with ineligibility for reelection. But in 1805, Jefferson wrote to John Taylor declaring, with a modified view, that service for eight years was better suited to his experience. Jefferson was then serving in his fifth year as President. Andrew Jackson, James K. Polk, William Henry Harrison, Andrew Johnson, Grover Cleveland, and William Howard Taft advocated, at one time or another, the six-year term. In fact, the average length of time that a President serves in the White House is five years. Thus history, tradition, even experience, are not offended by this proposed change. . . ."

SENATE JOINT RESOLUTIONS 19, 20, AND 21—ELECTORAL REFORM
—THE AIKEN-MANSFIELD PROPOSALS

(Submitted into the record from the Congressional Record of *January 17, 1969)*

MR. AIKEN: Mr. President, as a Member of the Senate, I have served under six Presidents—two Republicans and four Democrats.

Each of them contributed much to the growth and welfare of our country.

Each of them made mistakes.

They all had one thing in common.

Each wanted to be a good President.

Quite naturally each wanted to be the best President we ever had.

And, hopefully perhaps, on my part I wanted each one to be the best.

They had another thing in common.

With the possible exception of President Eisenhower, each one was assailed and harassed not only by members of the opposite party but also by dissatisfied members of his own party.

In some instances, we might say that the opposition they engendered was warranted and contributed to the security and prosperity of the country.

In other instances, it may be said that harassment and embarrassment of the President was politically motivated and has proved costly to the people of America.

We have only one President at a time and the manner in which he conducts the duties of his office determines to a great degree whether the people of the United States are secure or insecure—prosperous or poor —happy or sad.

With this overweening belief in mind, I have to the best of my ability tried to help to serve this country well—regardless of party.

Each President I have known has, to a great extent, been at the mercy of the times during which he served.

Each has had to establish and maintain his credibility in the field of international politics, with varying degrees of success.

And upon the success of the President in making the right decisions and in maintaining the respect of the world rested the prestige of our Nation and of you and me in the eyes of the world.

Temptation and desire are hardy and ruthless characters—possessed by all of us in varying degrees.

Each of us wants to be important, and in order to be important we seek power.

There are many kinds of power eyed by our ambition—economic, social, political and, in some cases, racial. . . .

I am making this statement to call attention to the indisputable fact that no President can give his best to the Nation or maintain our prestige in the world so long as he is constantly being fired upon by those whose principal purpose is to keep him from being reelected. . . .

The one-term limitation has worked well in other countries.

It permits the President to devote all his time and efforts to the service of his country.

This constitutional amendment would go far in discouraging would-be successors to the office from wasting their time in harassing him or trumping up unwarranted charges or impeding his work because he could not run against any of them anyway.

Mr. President, I hope that this Congress will seriously consider the amendment proposed by Senator Mansfield and myself.

MR. MANSFIELD: Mr. President, will the Senator yield?

MR. AIKEN: I yield.

MR. MANSFIELD: Let me say that I am delighted that the dean of the Republicans has indicated his strong support for the resolution which he and I introduced some months ago. We think it is a way to allow any President—regardless of party—to be himself and not to be subject to political harassments. It is a way that allows the President to assume his office with one purpose in mind—to do a good job, regardless of the consequences, and then to depart. . . .

COMMENT

(Submitted into the record from Harper's Weekly, *May 11, 1912)*

"*The Clayton Resolution* — It provides, in brief, that the following be adopted by the Congress and the states as a substitute for Section I. of Article II. of the Constitution of the United States:

" 'The executive power shall be vested in a President of the United States of America. He shall hold his office during the term of six years and shall be ineligible to a second term.'

"This is in substance the provision which James Madison urged upon the Constitutional Convention, which Thomas Jefferson pleaded for in letters to George Washington, which Andrew Jackson recommended in four distinct messages to Congress, and which, on December 15, 1875, a Democratic House of Representatives approved in spirit without a dissenting vote from any member of the historic party.

"The reasons for the acceptance of the amendment are so potent and so obvious that they hardly require to be set forth. A few, however, may be stated briefly.

"It will remove the living menace of Caesarism.

"It will enhance enormously the efficiency of a President, first, by removing the temptation and recognized need of seeking a renomination, and, secondly, by according to him sufficient time to make effective the purposes for which he was chosen.

"It will kill the base use of political patronage and induce inevitably a higher standard of appointments.

"It will make impossible a repetition of the humiliating spectacle of a President of the United States forced to the hustings in defense of his administration's conduct, his party's integrity, and his own personal honor.

"It will reduce by one-half the tremendous losses consequent upon a turbulent national election.

"It will save to the country directly millions of dollars, and to the people indirectly hundreds of millions.

"It will enable a President to be President, and not an office-seeker; a statesman, and not a politician; a true servant, not of a faction, but of the whole people, freed to heed the dictates of conscience and judgment, and ambitious only to achieve fair and honorable fame.

"It will show that the people *can* amend their Constitution when occasion requires. . . ."

PROPOSED AMENDMENTS TO THE CONSTITUTION OF THE UNITED STATES
ADVOCATING ONE PRESIDENTIAL TERM OF
6 YEARS

(Submitted into the record by the Legislative Reference Service of the Library of Congress)

Congress, Session, and Resolution	Introduced By	Date of Introduction
19th, 1st	Hemphill	Feb. 24, 1826
20th, 2d	Smyth	Dec. 18, 1828
Do	Condict	Feb. 7, 1829
22d, 1st	Root	Mar. 2, 1832
23d, 2d	Speight	Feb. 25, 1835
24th, 2d	Galbraith	Dec. 29, 1836
29th, 1st, S. 8	Bagley	Jan. 21, 1846
38th, 1st, S. 16	Powell	Apr. 6, 1864
39th, 2d, S. 33	Poland	Feb. 11, 1867
42d, 2d, H.R. 49	Potter	Dec. 6, 1871
42d, 3d, H.R. 163	Banks	Dec. 9, 1872
43d, 1st, S. 2	Summer	Dec. 1, 1873
43d, 2d, H.R. 124	Storm	Dec. 14, 1874
44th, 1st, H.R. 2	Randall	Dec. 14, 1875
44th, 1st, H.R. 6	Harrison	Do.
44th, 1st, H.R. 7	Morrison	Do.
44th, 1st, H.R. 47	Potter	
44th, 1st, H.R. 41	Frye	Jan. 18, 1876
44th, 1st, H.R. 62	Oliver	Feb. 7, 1876
45th, 1st, H.R. 36	House	Nov. 6, 1877
45th, 2d, H.R. 65	Joyce	Dec. 10, 1877
46th, 1st, H.R. 67	Buckner	May 13, 1879
48th, 1st, S. 74	Jackson	Mar. 12, 1884
48th, 2d, H.R. 299	Millard	Dec. 12, 1884

Congress, Session, and Resolution	Introduced By	Date of Introduction
49th, 1st, S. 11	Jackson	Dec. 15, 1885
49th, 1st, H.R. 69	Millard	Jan. 7, 1886
49th, 1st, H.R. 107	McCreary	Feb. 1, 1886
50th, 1st, H.R. 149	McCorns	Apr. 16, 1886
50th, 1st, H.R. 167	Neal	May 14, 1888
51st, 1st, H.R. 35	McCorns	Dec. 18, 1889
51st, 1st, H.R. 101	Taylor	Feb. 17, 1890
52d, 1st, H.J. Res. 33	Stewart	Jan. 7, 1892
52d, 1st, H.J. Res. 82	Springer	Feb. 8, 1892
52d, 1st, S.J. Res. 53	Proctor	Feb. 18, 1892
53d, 1st, H.J. Res. 23	Beltzhoover	Sept. 6, 1893
53d, 2d, H.J. Res. 111	Oates	Jan. 15, 1894
54th, 1st, S.J. Res. 9	Peffer	Dec. 3, 1895
54th, 2d, S.J. Res. 180	Proctor	Dec. 21, 1896
56th, 1st, H.J. Res. 11	Fitzgerald	Dec. 4, 1899
56th, 1st, S.J. Res. 30	Harris	Dec. 7, 1899
56th, 1st, H.J. Res. 223	Aldrich	Mar. 30, 1900
58th, 1st, H.J. Res. 32	Gaines	Nov. 16, 1903
58th, 3d, S.J. Res. 87	Bailey	Jan. 5, 1905
59th, 1st, H.J. Res. 2	Gaines	Dec. 4, 1905
59th, 2d, S.J. Res. 77	Cullom	Dec. 7, 1906
59th, 2d, H.J. Res. 197	Lowden	Dec. 10, 1906
60th, 1st, H.J. Res. 65	do	Dec. 16, 1907
60th, 1st, H.J. Res. 67	Hamilton	Dec. 19, 1907
60th, 1st, S.J. Res. 16	Cullom	Dec. 21, 1907
60th, 1st, H.J. Res. 85	Granger	Jan. 6, 1908
60th, 2d, S.J. Res. 110	Dillingham	Jan. 4, 1909
61st, 1st, H.J. Res. 11	Lowden	Mar. 15, 1909
61st, 1st, S.J. Res. 15	Cullom	Apr. 5, 1909
62d, 2d, H.J. Res. 237	Higgins	Feb. 5, 1912
62d, 2d, S.J. Res. 78	Works	Feb. 13, 1912
62d, 2d, H.J. Res. 248	Curley	Feb. 21, 1912
62d, 2d, H.J. Res. 311	Clayton	Apr. 30, 1912
62d, 2d, H.J. Res. 313	do	May 1, 1912
63d, 2d, H.J. Res. 325	do	June 13, 1912
63d, 3d, H.J. Res. 364	DeForest	Dec. 3, 1912
63d, 1st, S.J. Res. 11	Works	Apr. 8, 1913
63d, 1st, H.J. Res. 45	Barkley	Do.
63d, 1st, S.J. Res. 21	Thompson	Apr. 17, 1913
63d, 1st, H.J. Res. 78	Curley	Apr. 29, 1913
63d, 1st, H.J. Res. 86	Britten	May 16, 1913
63d, 1st, H.J. Res. 94	Rucker	June 6, 1913
63d, 1st, H.J. Res. 97	do	June 17, 1913
63d, 1st, H.J. Res. 106	Madden	July 12, 1913
63d, 2d, H.J. Res. 345	Buchanan	Sept. 11, 1914
63d, 3d, H.J. Res. 402	Beakes	Jan. 15, 1915
64th, 1st, H.J. Res. 34	do	Dec. 6, 1915
64th, 1st, S.J. Res. 23	Works	Dec. 7, 1915
64th, 1st, H.J. Res. 121	Barkley	Jan. 28, 1916
64th, 1st, H.J. Res. 122	Hayes	Jan. 29, 1916
64th, 1st, H.J. Res. 192	Bailey	Mar. 29, 1916
64th, 2d, S.J. Res. 177	Shafroth	Dec. 5, 1916
65th, 1st, H.J. Res. 120	Steele	July 11, 1917
66th, 2d, S.J. Res. 209	Smith	June 2, 1920

Congress, Session, and Resolution	Introduced By	Date of Introduction
67th, 1st, S.J. Res. 86	Harris	July 21, 1921
67th, 2d, H.J. Res. 290	Wood	Mar. 20, 1922
67th, 4th, H.J. Res. 413	Lineberger	Dec. 16, 1922
68th, 1st, S.J. Res. 6	Harris	Dec. 6, 1923
68th, 1st, H.J. Res. 185	Lineberger	Feb. 14, 1924
70th, 1st, H.J. Res. 88	Deal	Dec. 12, 1927
72d, 2d, H.J. Res. 599	Christopherson	Feb. 21, 1933
72d, 2d, H.J. Res. 608	Ramseyer	Do.
72d, 2d, H.J. Res. 96	McLean	Mar. 16, 1933
74d, 2d, H.J. Res. 423	Fletcher	Jan 3, 1936
75th, 1st, S.J. Res. 2	Burke	Jan. 6, 1937
75th, 1st, H.J. Res. 7	Culkin	Jan. 5, 1937
75th, 1st, H.J. Res. 15	Crowther	Do.
75th, 1st, H.J. Res. 37	Fletcher	Do.
75th, 1st, H.J. Res. 68	McLean	Do.
75th, 1st, H.J. Res. 70	Tinkham	Do.
76th, 1st, S.J. Res. 15	Burke	Jan. 4, 1939
76th, 1st, S.J. Res. 141	Wiley	May 31, 1939
76th, 1st, H.J. Res. 40	Culkin	Jan. 3, 1939
76th, 1st, H.J. Res. 43	Crowther	Do.
76th, 1st, H.J. Res. 50	McLean	Do.
76th, 1st, H.J. Res. 312	Angell	June 5, 1939
77th, 1st, S.J. Res. 13	Wiley	Jan. 8, 1941
77th, 1st, H.J. Res. 4	Angell	Jan. 3, 1941
77th, 1st, H.J. Res. 9	Crowther	Do.
77th, 1st, H.J. Res. 12	Culkin	Do.
77th, 1st, H.J. Res. 87	Tinkham	Jan. 24, 1941
78th, 1st, S.J. Res. 86	O'Daniel	Oct. 14, 1943
78th, 1st, H.J. Res. 25	Angell	Jan. 6, 1943
78th, 1st, H.J. Res. 130	Dondero	May 25, 1943
78th, 1st, H.J. Res. 172	Arnold	Oct. 14, 1943
79th, 1st, S.J. Res. 21	O'Daniel	Jan. 22, 1945
79th, 1st, H.J. Res. 36	Dondero	Jan. 3, 1945
79th, 1st, H.J. Res. 68	Angell	Jan. 15, 1945
79th, 1st, H.J. Res. 151	Lemke	Apr. 12, 1945
79th, 1st, H.J. Res. 229	Arnold	July 17, 1945
79th, 2d, H.J. Res. 339	Randolph	Apr. 13, 1946
80th, 1st, S.J. Res. 18	O'Daniel	Jan. 8, 1947
80th, 1st, S.J. Res. 29	Fulbright	Jan. 15, 1947
80th, 1st, S.J. Res. 55	Bridges	Feb. 3, 1947
80th, 1st, H.J. Res. 4	Angell	Jan. 3, 1947
80th, 1st, H.J. Res. 6	Dondero	Do.
80th, 1st, H.J. Res. 25	Dirksen	Do.
80th, 1st, H.J. Res. 28	Mundt	Do.
80th, 1st, H.J. Res. 87	Lemke	Jan. 27, 1947
80th, 1st, H.J. Res. 111	Stockman	Feb. 6, 1947
81st, 1st, H.J. Res. 207	do	Mar. 29, 1949
82d, 1st, H.J. Res. 124	Angell	Jan. 22, 1951
82d, 1st, H.J. Res. 220	Stockman	Apr. 3, 1951
90th, 2d, S.J. Res. 178	Mansfield	June 17, 1968
91st, 1st, S.J. Res. 21	Mansfield, Aiken	Jan. 17, 1969
92d, 1st, S.J. Res. 77	do	Apr. 1, 1971
92d, 1st, H.J. Res. 736	Frenzel	June 22, 1971
92d, 1st, H.J. Res. 783	Chamberlain	July 15, 1971

Appendix E

The Nixon Group*

Bertram H. Raven
University of California, Los Angeles

(*The following excerpt is taken by permission from the* Journal of
Social Issues, *Volume 30, Number 4, 1974.*)

Signs of Power in Westwood Park

The sign, located on Veteran Avenue just south of Wilshire
Boulevard in West Los Angeles, reads in bold letters: "Westwood
Park Coming Soon." It has stood for several years now (since the
formal dedication by national, state, and local dignitaries) in front
of an old, cracked, asphalt parking lot behind the West Los Angeles
Federal Building. It announces further that this federal property
has been deeded to the city of Los Angeles for development of a
beautiful new green recreation area. In a new apartment house,
directly across from Westwood Park, lives my good friend and col-
league Jacqueline D. Goodchilds, the current editor of the *Journal
of Social Issues.* I am deeply indebted to Dr. Goodchilds for the
observations which follow. For, understandably, Dr. Goodchilds
and the other residents of the apartment house have been patiently
watching the cracked asphalt park with fond anticipation. How
often these days does one see asphalt changing into green lawns and
trees! Alas, the only signs of greenery they had seen in Westwood
Park as of July 1974 were occasional growths of tumbleweed and

*Originally entitled "The Power of Signs and the Signs of Power," this article was the
Presidential Address to the Society for the Psychological Study of Social Issues (SPSSI),
Division 9 of The American Psychological Association, presented at the annual meeting in
New Orleans, August 1974.

sedges, pushing up boldly through the cracks in the asphalt. But soon this would change.

The first signs of activity appeared in the afternoon of July 29 when a workman placed a number of yellow "No Parking" pylons around a large section of the asphalt lot. The next morning at 7:30 a number of workers appeared with a bulldozer, two trucks, a streetroller, and a sweeper. The bulldozer removed the plants and weeds that had been growing through the cracked asphalt, the roller made a number of runs over the asphalt to straighten it out, the street sweeper spent several hours washing the lot and sweeping it. It seemed rather strange, thought Dr. Goodchilds, that the construction of the park involved smoothing and cleaning the asphalt rather than removing it, but surely there must be some broader plan involved.

A bit later in the morning a great number of automobiles of differing color, make, and model year began to converge on the lot. From each auto emerged two men dressed in white T-shirts and blue trousers. They appeared to be workmen beginning the next phase of the park construction. But very soon the workmen donned blue uniforms, hats, badges, and guns and were transformed into policemen. They lined up in military formation, ten across, fifteen rows, 150 in total. The commanding officer gave them a briefing. Some then dispersed, others took positions at various edges of the parking lot. A dozen got into 5 or 6 of the private cars which had brought them to the spot and began cruising around the area.

It was now noon and the first group of SWAT officers arrived —the Special Weapons And Tactics force. The SWATs were dressed in armored uniforms, flak vests, and helmets and carried automatic rifles.

1:30 P.M. There now appeared on the rooftops of several surrounding apartment buildings a number of SWAT officers with field glasses and walkie-talkies in addition to their armament. To check out her observations, Dr. Goodchilds took out her own field glasses and boldly exchanged magnified glances with one of the men on the rooftops. Within the next hour the Fire Department appeared: hook-and-ladder truck, two pumpers, and a rescue ambulance. The hook-and-ladder was parked between the buildings out of sight and hoses were brought out at the ready—firemen standing by in helmets and raincoats. A motorcycle escort appeared —18 motorcycles, accompanying ten limousines with flags and official looking seals. There followed a brief moment of tense waiting. By now it was 4 o'clock and the first helicopter appeared, landing and taking off several times. It bore the markings of the L.A. City Police. Finally, low over the roof tops came an olive-drab army helicopter which landed and disgorged a number of men in civilian clothes. They turned out to be members of the press. Next appeared a large helicopter emblazoned with a red number 2, and at last, an even more important helicopter (number 1!) out of which emerged the 37th President of the United States, Richard M. Nixon. The president, of course, was accompanied by various dignitaries, including several high-ranking military officers. One such officer followed the president off the helicopter. He carried a small black box which, on contemplation, proved to be the most awe-inspiring object in this entire fantastic spectacle. It was of course the box which contained the supersecret codes, the push-button by which a president could trigger or suspend an all-out nuclear war. The box, if it must be referred to, has been called the "black bag" or the "football." The officer carrying it is called "the man with the satchel"—during the Kennedy administration he was also called "the bagman" [Manchester, 1967]. Presumably they don't call him that any more.

As the president in his limousine with the presidential seal and his entourage in their accompanying limousines roared away with their motorcycle escort, Dr. Goodchilds considered the fantastic expense—tens of thousands of dollars which the taxpayers must be putting out for the president's brief visit to our city. Soon the party had arrived at the Century Plaza Hotel where President Nixon gave what turned out to be his last official public address as president of the United States. The content of that address is now generally forgotten. It had something to do with how the United States should attempt to assume fiscal responsibility by reducing government expenditures.

The description of the Westwood Park scene triggers off a pattern of vivid associations for me, as it must for you. My associations include: POMP . . . EXTRAVAGANCE . . . SECURITY . . . IN-SECURITY . . . SECRECY . . . ISOLATION . . . LONELINESS . . . POWER . . .

Index

About the Author
(see p. 141)

Edward A. Morris, an attorney, is a former Alumni Regent of the University of California. While a Regent, he was Vice-Chairman of the committee overseeing the research laboratories which develop America's nuclear weapons.

Mr. Morris's writings are published in both legal and scientific journals. He was an active member of Business Executives for Peace in Vietnam, and also served on a regional advisory board of Amnesty International.

A native of Springfield, Illinois, Mr. Morris was an Air Force navigator during World War II. He earned a B.A. in economics from the University of California at Santa Barbara in 1950, and received his J.D. degree in 1953 from Hastings College of the Law in San Francisco, where he now resides with his wife Betty.